COGNITIVE BEHAVIORAL THERAPY COMPLETE GUIDE

Help yourself understanding the thoughts and feelings that influence behaviors. Overcome disorders, phobias, addictions, depression, and anxiety.

By

Frederick L. Begs

monetary loss due to the information herein, either directly or indirectly.

Respective authors own all copyrights not held by the publisher.

The information herein is offered for informational purposes solely, and is universal as so. The presentation of the information is without contract or any type of guarantee assurance.

The trademarks that are used are without any consent, and the publication of the trademark is without permission or backing by the trademark owner. All trademarks and brands within this book are for clarifying purposes only and are the owned by the owners themselves, not affiliated with this document.

ISBN: 9781704010472

WHY YOU SHOULD READ THIS BOOK

What is emotional mastery? Emotions are often described as energy in motion. They become problems only when we judge them as wrong, bad, or inappropriate. When we let our emotions run us, we miss the message that they carry. When we stuff them down for fear of what they might cause us to do, they simply lie in wait to emerge with a vengeance later on. Emotional mastery is the ability to process our emotions so that we receive their message and use their energy for appropriate action.

Our emotions are a reflection of our beliefs about life events. For example, if you believe that you are your work and you suddenly lose your job, you are likely to feel an incredible amount of fear, as you perceive your very survival to be at stake. If you repress this fear, you'll probably experience anger or rage and at some point, you will likely lash out at whoever s available.

If on the other hand, you are a person who views your job simply as one aspect of your life, and you know that your inherent value lies in your unique skills and qualities, then your feelings and response to losing your job will probably be a whole lot different. You may just view this loss as an opportunity to explore a whole new path for yourself.

The bottom line here is this: how you feel in any situation corresponds exactly with what you believe about yourself and the situation. Master your beliefs, and you'll master your emotions.

Knowing that you can change how you feel simply by changing how you think about each experience is a powerful concept. If you feel upset about something, ask yourself, "How can I reinterpret this event in a such a way that I can feel good or at least OK about it?" If you have a bill you can't pay for example, instead of getting upset, decide that this is an opportunity to redesign your financial life. Ask for help, develop a plan, and use your energy to get moving on it.

How you think about your emotions adds another layer. We often give ourselves a double whammy when we get upset about feeling upset. Here are some positive ways to interpret the purpose of our basic emotions, set down by Peter McWilliams in his book, "Do It."

- Fear is the energy to do your best in a new situation.

- Guilt is the energy for personal change-it is anger directed toward ourselves, and anger is the energy for change.

- Unworthiness keeps us on track--just as we can have anything we want, we can't have everything we want. So too, we are worthy of anything we want, but we may not be worthy of everything we want.

- Hurt feelings are a reminder of how much we care.

So how can you use this information in your life? I suggest that you examine any beliefs you hold around emotions and the situations that trigger them.

Begin to cultivate present moment awareness as your emotions arise. Just notice them and look at them, not as good or bad, but simply with curiosity, and with the question, what's this energy for and how do I choose to use it?

Practice. Begin the practice of observing emotions when they arise and identify any judgments you might have about them.

Focus instead on listening to the message they hold for you. Then, act on this message by expressing the emotion in a positive fashion.

It might seem difficult to cure panic attack, but there are several ways to treat it so that attacks are much less likely to occur. There is no known cause for this disorder, but there are a few factors that are believed to contribute to it. Stress and genetics have been associated with panic attacks. There's not much you can do about genetics, but there are plenty of ways to change how you respond to stress.

The other main factor involves how your brain reacts in situations that make you tense or anxious. Instead of having a rational response, your brain causes your body to go into the "fight or flight" mode. This defensive reaction leads to panic attack symptoms such as increased heart rate, troubled breathing, chest pain, and faintness. Changing how your brain responds is trickier than learning how to handle stress, but it can be accomplished.

In order to retrain your brain, psychotherapy is usually suggested as a cure for panic attack. Cognitive behavioral therapy helps you develop new thought patterns to replace the ones that lead to attacks in the first place. If a certain situation causes you to become anxious, this type of therapy will have you redirect your thoughts to something you consider non-threatening or pleasant in order to fend off an attack. By doing this, you are associating these new, positive images with the stressful situation instead of focusing on the negative image that causes you to panic.

The main advantage to this form of treatment is that you can learn to recognize what makes you nervous or anxious so that you're better able to deal with these situations. Therapy will also show you how to cope with this anxiety if you have trouble getting rid of it altogether. Knowing that you will have the ability to face your fears and respond to them calmly can give you that much needed boost of confidence you need to prevent panic attacks.

TABLE OF CONTENTS

INTRODUCTION

How you handle stress can be a big indicator of whether or not you are likely to suffer from an attack. Arming yourself with techniques to combat stress and anxiety might not cure panic attack for good, but it can help you prevent attacks. There are a variety of stress management methods that teach you how to cope with anxiety while remaining calm and centered. By focusing on these methods, you can distract your brain from reacting irrationally to stress. Yoga, meditation, deep breathing, and guided imagery are some of the techniques that you can use to accomplish this.

Dealing with stress is a good way to reduce anxiety and lessen your chances of having panic attacks, while teaching your brain to respond differently in certain situations is an effective way to cure panic attack. If you don't have the time and money to spend on therapy sessions, then fortunately there are home remedies that can help you achieve this cure. They work much more quickly and efficiently and will enable you to live calmly and happily without having to worry about having panic attacks.

As its name implies, cognitive behavioral therapy

deals primarily in two areas of psychology:

Cognitive - thoughts, the inner workings of the mind

Behavioral - actions, what a person does, how a person reacts to a situation

Developed in the 1960s by a group of professionals, cognitive behavioral therapy (CBT) merged two separate therapies to create a dynamic model to help clients. Behavior therapy and cognitive therapy were used separately mostly until they were merged together.

CBT's basis of thoughts and actions working together helps bring to light the fact that actions and behaviors are not determined by externalities, but by thoughts. Using this theory, CBT has been able to help many clients overcome false beliefs about themselves as well as improve quality of life.

Cognitive behavioral therapy has been found effective in many different mental disorders. Not only is it used for depression and self-esteem or self-worth issues, CBT has been proven highly effective in other mental disorders such as:

- Schizophrenia

- Bipolar disorder

- Anxiety disorders

- Insomnia

- Post-traumatic stress disorder

- Mood disorders

CBT is more than just the combination of two separate therapies, it enables client and therapist to collaborate, form a relationship of trust and resolve complex issues. CBT helps clients find the true reason(s) and thought(s) that are driving their action(s), approaches them productively and helps clients transform their thought processes to create more rational reactions to dangerous situations.

Cognitive behavioral therapy has more benefits than just pin-pointing from where behaviors originate, CBT is much more streamlined and takes less time than traditional therapy. Its general timeline consists of about sixteen (16) sessions while other traditional therapies can last for years.

Cognitive behavioral therapy enables clients to react more effectively to life situations. It enables them to live life to its fullest potential without fear of possible irrational reactions to triggering situations. It creates for clients the ability to think and act rationally, think before acting and determine the best course of action for any given situation.

CBT is effective in many different areas of the psychology spectrum. It is proven to work quickly and effectively.

Cognitive behavioral therapy is an approach used by psychotherapists to influence a patient's behaviors and emotions. The key to the approach is in its procedure which must be systematic. It has been used successfully to treat a variety of disorders including eating disorders, substance abuse, anxiety and personality disorders. It can be used in individual or group therapy sessions and the approach can also be geared towards self help therapy.

Cognitive behavioral therapy is a combination of traditional behavioral therapy and cognitive therapy. They are combined into a treatment that is focused on symptom removal. The effectiveness of the treatment can clearly be judged based on its results. The more it is used, the more it has become recommended. It is now used as the number one treatment technique for post-traumatic stress disorder, obsessive compulsive disorder, depression and bulimia.

Cognitive behavioral therapy first began to be used between 1960 and 1970. It was a gradual process of merging behavioral therapy techniques and cognitive therapy techniques. Behavioral therapy had been around since the 1920's, but cognitive therapy was not introduced until the

4

1960's. Almost immediately the benefits of combining it with behavioral therapy techniques were realized. Ivan Pavlov, with his dogs who salivated at the ringing of the dinner bell, was among the most famous of the behavioral research pioneers. Other leaders in the field included John Watson and Clark Hull.

Instead of focusing on analyzing the problem like Freud and the psychoanalysts, cognitive behavioral therapy focused on eliminating the symptoms. The idea being that if you eliminate the symptoms, you have eliminated the problem. This more direct approach was seen as more effective at getting to the problem at hand and helping patients to make progress more quickly.

As a more radical aggressive treatment, behavioral techniques dealt better with more radical problems. The more obvious and clear cut the symptoms were, the easier it was to target them and devise treatments to eliminate them. Behavioral therapy was not as successful initially with more ambiguous problems such as depression. This realm was better served with cognitive therapy techniques.

In many academic settings, the two therapy techniques were used side by side to compare and contrast the results. It was not long before the advantages of combining the two techniques became clear as a way of taking advantage of the strengths of each. David Barlow's work on panic disorder treatments provided the first concrete example of the success of the combined strategies.

Cognitive behavioral therapy is difficult to define in a succinct definition because it covers such a broad range of topics and techniques. It is really an umbrella definition for individual treatments that are specifically tailored to the problems of a specific patient. So the problem dictates the specifics of the treatment, but there are some common themes and techniques. These include having the patient keep a diary of important events and record the feelings and behaviors they had in association with each event. This tool is then used as a basis to analyze and test the patient's ability to evaluate the situation and develop an appropriate emotional response. Negative emotions and behaviors are identified as well as the evaluations and beliefs that lead to them. An effort is then made to counter these beliefs and evaluations to show that the resulting behaviors are wrong. Negative behaviors are eliminated and the patient is taught a better way to view and react to the situation.

Part of the therapy also includes teaching the patient ways to distract themselves or change their focus from something that is upsetting or a situation that is generating negative behavior. They learn to focus on something else instead of the negative stimulus, thus eliminating the negative behavior that it would lead to. The problem is essentially nipped in the bud. For serious psychological disorders like bipolar disorder or schizophrenia, mood stabilizing medications are often prescribed to use in conjunction with these techniques. The medications give the patient enough of a calming effect to give them the opportunity to examine the situation and make the healthy choice whereas before they could not even pause for rational thought.

Cognitive behavioral therapy has been proven effective for a variety of problems, but it is still a process, not a miracle cure. It takes time to teach patients to understand situations and identify the triggers of their negative behaviors. Once this step is mastered, it still takes a lot of effort to overcome their first instincts and instead stop and make the right choices. First they learn what they should do, and then they must practice until they can do it.

In today's ever changing world, we sometimes need help to get rid of habits and calm our fears. We can turn to the traditional methods: doctors, government agencies and over the counter medication. We can talk to therapists and psychologists. We can even go-it-alone. Sometimes, however, when it seems nothing we do is helping our situation, we need a little help that is outside the box. It is time to consider self-hypnosis. It can work where all other methods have let us down.

What is Self Hypnosis?

Self-hypnosis is a relative of hypnosis. It simply replaces a hypnotherapist or other qualified individual with the client. In other words, the hypnotist is also the client. Self-hypnosis, like hypnosis, is tool of self-discovery and awareness. It is a means through which anyone can access the subconscious mind. You do so deliberately with the intent to alter the current pattern of thought held by the subconscious. In doing so, you begin to lay the groundwork for change.

The Purpose of Self Hypnosis

The purpose of Self-hypnosis varies in accordance with the individual's needs. The basic function of this technique is to help an individual reach deep down into his or her subconscious. In doing so, you can retrain it to reflect and embrace what you wish to accomplish. Some typical purposes of self-hypnosis include:

- To quit smoking

- To help with a diet

- To improve your overall self-image

- To help you overcome any fears

- To stop such things as procrastination

- To aid you in addressing phobias

- To assist you in improving your memory

- How does Self Hypnosis Differ from Stage Hypnosis?

Hypnosis and self-hypnosis are respected forms of therapy. These forms of hypnotherapy are used to achieve a specific purpose - one in which only the person desiring change or seeking a solution and the therapist take part. The goals the therapist and client set are individualistic and meant to address a real need. The sessions and subjects are personal, private and performed in a safe and secure environment. If you use self-hypnosis, only you need to know why you are there.

In the case of stage hypnosis, the major difference is the stage. This is a public performance. People have paid the hypnotist/magician to see what he or she can "make" someone do. The "client" or stage prop is not there to achieve any personal goal except, perhaps for their few minutes of fame. The stage hypnotist can be manipulative and even exploitative to obtain his or her goals. Moreover, the whole strategy requires more than a little of illusion and even self-delusion.

The Tools of Self Hypnosis

The tools you use are basic. You need a quiet place - particularly essential at the beginning. You need to create, purchase or download various audio aids. These contain basic scripts to help you reach your subconscious. They also contain the specific messages you wish your subconscious to accept.

You need to make some time for the session. This should occur on a regular, preferably daily, basis. The setting should not only be quiet but comfortable. It needs to feel safe.

You can, if you wish, light incense and/or candles. This adds to the atmosphere. It can be helpful in relaxing you. This increases the ability of you to reach your trance-like state more quickly.

The other tools for actual hypnosis lie within you. You need to be able to reach a trance-like state. You need to relax. You have to be specific in your goal. You need to then visualise it clearly and progressively. The timeframe of this goal must firmly resonate in your conscious and subconscious minds. It must be here, now and in the near future if it is to be effective. The Advantages of Self Hypnosis Self-hypnosis has several advantages over its formal hypnotherapy colleague. It is:

Inexpensive - you require many a few books and audio-visual aids, many obtainable online through downloads

For home use. It is nice to be able to relax in the safety and comfort of your own

Also portable when you feel comfortable doing so

Does not require setting up an appointment

You can do so at your own pace in your own time

In our modern world, we seem to find it harder to relax. Our lives are full of busyness and we are constantly bombarded with stressors; our minds are continually chattering and full of worry. What we often don't realize is this chronic state of mental unease is the beginning of disease in our body. When we are in this constant mental state of agitation, our body is on constant alert, our metabolic rate increases, our adrenal glands are on overdrive and our brains are giving the signal to pump out more cortisol (the degenerative hormone) into our blood.

Cortisol is important when we need to fight or take

flight, and it has helped us survive, but it is only good in small doses. Cortisol is very hard on our bodies and when we have too much of it in our blood, for too long, it accelerates our physical decline. Ageing us faster, it acts as a destructive agent. This is bad news. Because we have become habituated to a state of high alert, this same hormone we called upon to save us in emergencies, is now pumping through our bodies on a daily basis and accelerating our degeneration. In essence the high-pressure lifestyle of our age has put our bodies into self-destruct gear.

It is a fact that physical and mental illness is hitting people in ever increasing numbers and at much younger ages despite the fact that, as a species, we are the most resourceful and scientifically advanced civilization of human history. We also know, but habitually ignore the fact, that the mind is the gatekeeper of our health and wellbeing.

When scientists observe the activity of the brain during different mental states, it is clear that positive mental states create positive effects in the physical body. For example when in a state of deep relaxation or medi-tation, the brain enters what is commonly referred to as the delta brainwave state. This is the state of deep healing. While in this state, the brain sends signals to the body to release regenerative, ant-aging hormones (DHEA and Melatonin) into the blood serum while also giving the command to reduce the cortisol that gets released during high alert and stressed mental states.

Similarly, there have been numerous case studies where patients suffering potentially terminal illnesses where exposed to deep relaxation, and meditation techniques. Compared to the individuals of the control group those exposed to regular 'doses' of deep relaxation had either completely healed or extended their longevity substantially compared to those in the control group. What is conclusive is that time to relax deeply and ease our minds is crucial to our health, it is the antidote to the high-pressured lives most of us are living and without it, most of us will die younger than we need to.

A daily dose of deep relaxation, will not only improve your health, but will improve your overall mental state. As well as releasing regenerative hormones, being in a deeply relaxed state also releases endorphins and the 'happy' neurotransmitter serotonin. By adopting a daily practice to deeply relax, you will, in time, normalize yourself into a mentally happy state.

One of the most, or perhaps the most, effective way to achieve a state of deep relaxation is through meditation. Meditation is tranquility for the mind, and where the mind goes, the body follows. However meditation is a serious practice that does not suit everyone. If meditation does not appeal, there are other ways to achieve this, and one must find what suits best. Using relaxation, meditative or binaural beat recordings are a proven, easy and effective choice. Alternatively, yoga, or tai chi might suit better. Whichever means one decides upon is secondary to the result, what is most important is that the technique used causes the brain to slow down its brainwave frequency where the damage of a high gear life can be reversed.

Things That Hypnosis Can Help

1) Anger management

Hypnosis can be used to directly treat anger issues, for example if a person is prone to throwing fits of rage, they can be pacified; using hypnotism the person can be trained into automatically calming themselves before signs of fury start to show. Hypnosis can also be used to treat anger problems by resolving any underlying problems such as high stress levels or lack of sleep.

2) Depression

It is estimated that one in four people will end up being treated for depression in their lifetime. Hypnosis can be used to communicate with the sufferer's unconscious mind and encourage a more upbeat demeanour and attitude while discouraging thoughts which may lead to a progression in their condition.

3) Pain

Pain is just in the mind, though it is a useful tool as it helps to detect issues in the body. However as everybody knows pain is not just a boon. For example when a person has cancer they will still feel pain as their mind expects then to be able to cure the condition (which is basically not possible). In this case the best option is to manage the pain; there are many options available for this. Hypnosis is very effective for dealing with, and is sometimes favourable than other options as it is completely un-invasive.

4) Fears

Fears and phobias are a construct of the mind. They are one of two things; innate (we are born with them; or learned from the surrounding and environment. Regardless of where they come from hypnosis is a very effective treatment, and in fact can be better than other methods in some cases. For example complex fears such as a fear of failure should be treated with hypnosis as it can't be treated with the most conventional method: flooding, which involves exposing the sufferer to an extreme amount of the thing they're afraid of in the hope that they will become desensitised. However this is neigh impossible to do with a fear of failure as the person can't be flooded with failing... Fortunately there is hypnosis.

5) Nerves

One of the stages in clinical hypnosis is called deepening. This involves completely relaxing the patients entire body. During this stage patients are so relaxed that any nerves or worries that they have will seem oblivious and insignificant. In some cases if the patient has gone to see a hypnotherapist to treat an illness and they happen to have nerves as well, they often find that after the treatment is finished the symptoms of nerves have also been alleviated.

6) Obsessive compulsive disorder (OCD)

The symptoms of OCD normally involve the patient repeating an action multiple times, for example a common action is to wash ones hands repeatedly. OCD can consume both a patient and their lives. It is considered a 'learned' condition that originates from the sufferer's childhood; in particular times of great stress the sufferer will perform the action to relieve stress. As it is a fairly severe condition many treatments have been developed, among them hypnosis. In the case of OCD hypnosis works by delving into the patient's unconscious and removing any links they have between the action (e.g.

washing hands) and the relief of stress thus encouraging them to find better ways of removing stress.

7) Alcoholism, smoking and other drug addictions

Similar to OCD addictions such as alcoholism are simply a psychological link between a stimulant (e.g. alcohol) and a positive feeling. However addictions aren't as deeply embedded into the mind. This means that they are far easier to treat and often can be done with self-hypnosis tapes as opposed to a trained hypnotherapist.

CHAPTER 1
ANXIETY DISORDER AND PANIC ATTACKS - HOW COGNITIVE BEHAVIOR THERAPY CAN HELP YOU

When a person out of the blue feels fearful it may well be the consequence of a combination of symptoms. This could be a panic attack, a type of anxiety disorder. These symptoms happen often with no evident causes. However research demonstrated that panic attacks can be triggered by medications, heredity, alcohol, drug withdrawal and serious disease. It happens frequently that people are unaware that they are having a panic attack. It may well last for as long as 20 minutes to as short as 10 seconds. The ailment and the symptoms can be treated with a range of remedies. There are two foremost approaches that medical doctors take are: one, by cognitive behavioral therapy; and two, by taking medications.

Lots of disorders and also anxiety disorders are cured with cognitive behavioral therapy (CBT). For panic attacks, CBT is used as the first line treatment and is the best treatment for people not responding to medications. With CBT, a psychotherapist helps a patient explore gradually to the grounds or reason of his fear. This is based on the assumption that anxiety of something is conditioned in someone's mind. Phobias are reinforced, when a sufferer constantly keeps away from the subject of his panic. As a result, not being frightened of the stimulus is what a person needs to learn. In this process, it is essential to discover how the patient deals with thoughts that cause alarm or anxiety. The therapist will begin giving information concerning the issue and how the cure is to be administered. Then the symptoms one would sense will be recreated in a controlled surrounding. This will be repeated up to five times a day for at least one minute. It can take weeks before a patient is not worried any longer by a sudden beginning of symptoms.

Cognitive behavioral therapy results in positive long terms effects to patients. Some patients can be seen with relative improvements in about six to eight weeks. It has also been known to prevent relapses for clients who have discontinued their medications. People who underwent cognitive behavioral therapy have a higher success rate when they discontinue taking benzodiazepine. When medications and cognitive behavioral therapy are combined it creates better results than when a person decides to use just one. Panic attacks are a severe disorder; for that reason it is best to check with one or two doctors before making use of any mode of therapy. Even if panic attacks can reoccur, they can be successfully cured.

A panic attack could at first appear like a terrifying experience, but treating the subsequent episodes should not be. With appropriate help from the medical doctor, a patient will be able to handle with its occurrence on his own.

Cognitive-behavioral therapy, or CBT, works on the patient's thoughts and behaviors in order to change how they feel and react to "negative" situations.

CBT is based on the assumption that the way we react to things is conditioned and that it can be changed by un-learning the conditioned responses.

CBT seeks to identify the thinking patterns that are negatively affecting the patient's life and to find more resourceful ways of thinking or self-talking. Examples of distorted forms of thinking include:

Should/must thinking: you turn your desires and pref-erences into absolute necessities. Some examples of this type of thinking include: "I have to get this", "This shouldn't have happened", "This person has to be nice to me".

Overgeneralization: you see a single undesirable event as permanent pattern of misfortune. For example: somebody does not treat you well and you think "I am never able to please people", even though the other person treated you bad because he or she was not in a good mood.

Magnification and minimization: you exaggerate the negatives and discount the positives. For example, you are driving and turn at the wrong location. Then you think: "I have a terrible sense of direction" or "I am such a bad driver", even though you rarely do a little "mistake" like this.

Mind-reading: you assume what other people are thinking about you without having real evidence for your assumption.

We can see that these forms of thinking cause anxiety. You may consider, inside you, that these thinking patterns valid, true or necessary. But you don't need to see them this way. We all see other people around us that behave calmly and do better in the situations described in the examples shown above, even though these situations happen to these people many more times than what we would personally consider acceptable. The way we react has more to do with our conditioned responses and beliefs than anything else.

Treatment with CBT is collaborative, due to the fact that the patient needs to apply the techniques indicated by the therapist in their day-to-day life. The actions to be done by the patient may include writing down a list of thoughts, emotions and behaviors that occurred after significant events in the patient daily routine. This list will be evaluated by the therapist to determine distorted thoughts and more resourceful ways of dealing with the particular problem. The therapy may also involve (gradual) imaginary exposure or real life exposure to a fear or phobic situation.

For CBT the cause of the problem is not relevant, because it focus on the "here and how", i.e., on the thoughts and behaviors that are causing or contributing to the problem

If you suffer from anxiety and panic attacks or depression, you probably heard "CBT for anxiety" mentioned many times. What is cognitive behavioral therapy? Why are there so many people talking about it? How can it permanently stop anxiety and panic attacks? This guide will answer all of these common questions.

What is Cognitive Behavioral Therapy?

CBT for anxiety is a form of therapy that concentrates on 2 connected things: Your cognition (your thoughts) and your behavior - your actions. You probably know that the way you think determines how you feel and the way you feel determines your actions and behavior. This is a "closed cycle" because your actions also influence how you feel.

You may not realize it, but your actions can create and elevate bad feelings.

Cognitive behavioral therapy teaches you how your thoughts and beliefs affect your feelings and how to change the way you think to eliminate bad feelings altogether.

How Can CBT Eliminate Your anxiety Attacks?

Most of us think that the situations we encounter and our everyday experiences are the triggers to anxiety, panic and depression. If you are driving your car, for instance, and when you get on a highway you get an anxiety attack, you probably think that your anxiety is caused by driving getting on the highway. This in not true. According to

CBT, your thoughts and set of beliefs determines the intensity of your emotions.

Cognitive behavioral therapy gives you simple techniques to stop panic and anxiety attacks dead in their tracks.

CBT is the only method that is able to cure anxiety and panic disorder permanently because it uses scientifically verified strategies to relieve anxiety for a long term. Other popular treatments - like medication, herbal remedies, breathing exercises and more - usually treat anxiety symptoms only and don't treat the root of the problem - Your brain and the way you think!

Although there are pharmaceutical drugs that are used to control anxiety disorders, not all are successful, and many produce unwanted side effects, including neurological damage, impotence, major weaknesses and addiction.

Cognitive Behavior Therapy (CBT) is an action-oriented, problem-solving therapy which has been found to be highly effective in treating anxiety and depressive disorders. This therapy is strategically devised to treat different problems in different individuals. CBT utilizes the "here and now" approach, emphasizing current life factors that maintain the problem, though past experiences that are directly relevant to the client's distress is welcomed into the discussion.

Cognitive-behavior therapists help clients to understand that although biological and environmental conditions can contribute to problems, the clients create, to a large degree, their own psychological disturbances and have the ability to significantly change these disturbances. Therapists play an integral part in correcting the disturbed evaluations, emotions, and behaviors of their clients by guiding them toward rational goals and purposes and assisting them in generating alternative courses of action.

Cognitive therapy helps clients to understand that distorted patterns of cognition have problematic emotional and behavioral consequences. Teaching clients to self-monitor their thoughts and feelings on a day-to-day basis through the utilization of a daily diary helps them unravel core beliefs and their relation to ongoing feelings and behaviors. In cognitive treatment, clients learn to detect and dispute their irrational beliefs by discriminating them from their rational alternatives. Over time, this enhanced awareness will lead them to actively challenge their dysfunctional thoughts by employing cognitive, emotive, and behavioral methods of change.

Behavior therapy assists clients in detecting behavioral patterns that are functionally related to the presenting complaint. A behavioral treatment plan is carefully tailored to meet each individual's needs and is dependent on the specific problem at hand. Often, techniques such as relaxation training and systematic desensitization are utilized to help clients gradually increase their comfort level in the presence of phobias or feared situations. In addition, modeling, behavior rehearsal, and planned exposures are some of the many tools that assist individuals in managing their anxieties more effectively.

The CBT therapist encourages the individual to be self-reliant and incorporates relapse prevention into treatment in order to maintain progress after discharge. The combination of a comprehensive CBT treatment, an empathic and supportive therapist, and motivated client is optimal in achieving notable improvements.

De-Constructing Cognitive Behavior Therapy (CBT)

When we de-construct the term, we look at each of the three words separately to increase our understanding of the whole.

Cognitive - from the Latin cogito I think.

Some of you might recall those Philosophy lectures about Rene Descartes and his famous 'cogito, ergo sum' -

I think, therefore I am. In general conversation, we link 'cognitive' with an intellectual engagement. We hear about cognitive deficits caused by brain damage, so let's say that the cognitive component of this therapy involves our brains, our thoughts. It explores how you think and react to things, and how those thoughts elicit an anxiety response or start your panic attacks. If you want to eliminate panic attacks, you have to recognize your role in creating and maintaining them via what I call unhelpful thinking, unhelpful habits of mind.

Behavioral or even behavioural

In this treatment model, the behavior component isn't just about how you behave in the sense of what you do. It's also about how you react before you do things, and it's also about how many of those behaviours become a habit and almost automatic. The behavioural component is also about the range of responses your therapists make available to you. Your therapist will work with you to find alternative ways to react, to break down your automatic responses. Through CBT, when you see that life (elevator) door opening, you'll be able to react in a calm way instead of automatically panicking about using the elevator. Cognitive Behaviour Therapy is an extremely interactive approach.

Therapy

The third part of CBT, therapy, is from the Greek therapeía healing. The healing or therapeutic component is about what you and your therapist do. It might involve you learning relaxation exercises, but it's also part of an ongoing conversation and series of observations about your thoughts, reactions and actions. Many therapists encourage daily meditation as part of helping clients to build up their reservoir of calm which is depleted daily by their hectic lives.

Eliminating Panic Attacks using Cognitive Behavior Therapy

Each anxiety or panic attack follows a well-documented cycle. In his very helpful book Facing Panic: Self Help for People with Panic Attacks Dr R Reid Wilson calls it The Panic Cycle. It's a cycle because one step seems to follow another much as the wheel of a bike goes around.

First step is where you have contact with a stimuli which makes you feel anything from slightly nervous to downright terrified. For instance, if you have had panic attacks in the shopping Mall, you'll feel terrified just entering those automatic doors.

In a Cognitive Behavior Therapy approach your therapist would have you look closely at that initial trigger. You may be asked to do something that seems paradoxical: you may be asked to increase the number of times you experience that initial fear. That's called an exposure-based intervention, and it can happen in your therapist's office or in the Mall. It's a way of allowing you to see what you already know at a rational level. Namely, that there is nothing to fear. Cognitive Behaviour Therapy allows you to think (cognitive) about your fear response (behavior) so that you can construct a more appropriate response (heal).

At the end of most panic attacks the anxiety reducing behaviour of choice is avoidance. You stay home, or you only go to the Mall with a friend who knows about your problem, or you only go to the movies if you can sit on the aisle seat - ready for a quick escape.

You're in charge. However, at both ends of the panic attacks cycle your reactions (cognitive responses) and be-haviour (panic or escaping) are the cause of your continuing discomfort. Both sets of behaviour are inappropriate. Both can be discussed as a way of re-writ-ing the script. What script? The one that says 'enter Mall, feel terrified'. It's your thoughts that evoke your adrenaline (fear) response. Through Cognitive Behaviour

Therapy, we can help you work with those thoughts and responses to re-align them so that you change your response to the automatic door at the Mall - or whatever triggers your fear.

There is a permanent cure for the wide range of anxiety conditions, including panic disorder, obsessive compulsive disorder, post-traumatic stress disorder, generalized anxiety disorder, social anxiety disorder, and phobias. According to the National Institute For Mental Health (NIMH), anxicty disorders plague 40 million American adults ages 18 and older. As we mull over significance of that staggering number, let's have a look at the recommended method of treatment, one that's provided recovery for hundreds of thousands of sufferers.

Cognitive behavioral therapy is actually a merging of two distinct therapies, both of which trace their roots back to the 1950s and 1960s-- and their acceptance by the medical establishment to the 1970s and 1980s.

Cognitive therapy was developed during the 1960s by American psychiatrist Aaron T. Beck. Beck originally applied his approach to matters of depression, then expanded his practice to include anxiety disorders. How it is that people interpret their daily lives and assign meaning is a process called cognition. Beck, disillusioned with traditional psychotherapeutic delving in to the subconscious, concluded that cognition, what his patients perceived, was the key to effective therapy that would lead to reliable recovery.

When developing his therapy, Beck first observed that depressed people adopt a negative perception of the world during formative years-- based on the loss of a loved one, peer rejection, criticism by authority figures, depressed attitudes present in significant others, plus a host of random negative events. Most often, this negative perception is fed and nurtured by a biased, emotional view of the world-- for example, all-or-nothing thinking, over-generalization, and selective perceptions that exclude vital, meaningful information. Cognitive therapy postulates that distortions in a person's perspectives grow into disorders. It is the job of a cognitive therapist to point out these distortions and encourage change in a sufferer's attitude.

Behavior therapy made its debut back in 1953, in the United States, in a research project headed by B.F. Skinner. In South Africa, Joseph Wolpe and his research group is credited with pioneering work. In the United Kingdom, Hans Eysenck contributed to the development of this type of therapy.

Behavior therapy relies primarily on functional analysis. Behavioral therapists has successfully been used as a treatment for intimacy problems, chronic pain, stress, anorexia, chronic distress, substance abuse, clinical depression and anxiety.

Behavior therapy is data-driven and contextual, concentrating on the environment and its context. Primarily, behavior therapy is concerned with the effect or consequence of a behavior, Behavior is viewed as statistically predictable, A person is treated as a whole, without the distractions of a mind versus body approach, but relationships, bidirectional interactions, are well taken into account.

Originally, anxiety conditions were viewed as byproducts of chemical imbalances and/or genetic predispositions. As these notions were abandoned, learned behaviors were credited as the source of most anxiety conditions. Hope for a permanent cure emerged, and, in the 1990s, cognitive therapy and behavioral therapy merged into cognitive behavioral therapy (CBT). The common ground for these two therapies is emphasis on the "here and and now" by focusing on alleviating symptoms and replacing harmful, self-destructive behavior with beneficial beliefs and attitudes.

In the United Kingdom, the National Institute for Health and Clinical Excellence recommends CBT as preferred treatment for mental health difficulties such as

OCD, post-traumatic stress disorder, bulimia, clinical depression, and even for the neurological condition chronic fatigue syndrome. In the United States, in spite of our obsession with pharmaceutical solutions, CBT has received acceptance within the medical establishment. Skilled, results-driven help is available for sufferers who seek it.

There you have it. The cat is out of the bag. Prescription medications? Not needed. A permanent cure for anxiety conditions? Within your grasp!

If you suffer from anxiety in any of its horrific manifestations, truly the best and most qualified person that you know is waiting for you to seek professional assistance by way of a licensed cognitive behavioral therapist. That person, always on your side, always to the rescue when you need it most, is you!

Anxiety medicines treat only the symptoms of the problem while CBT helps you target the root causes of the worries and fears associated with anxiety. The patient learns to relax and cope up with the thoughts leading to anxiety. Challenging your negative thoughts is an integral part of the therapy and is commonly known as cognitive restructuring. This helps you to assess your thought patterns which lead to negativity and an effort is made to replace them with positive and practical ideas. Three major steps involved in cognitive restructuring are:

Identification of negative thoughts: When a person suffers from anxiety disorder, they perceive circumstances more scary and devastating than they actually are. It is very important for them to distinguish between rational and irrational fears. A therapist helps to identify such impractical feelings.

Discarding the negative thoughts: Anxiety therapy teaches the individual to challenge his/her negative thoughts. Questioning and analyzing your beliefs, assessing the real situation and comparing it with your feelings helps to get rid of unwanted worries. After you realize that your anxiety is a result of mere hypothesis, you can discard your negative thoughts.

Learning to be practical: After a person has identified and discarded the negative feelings, he is ready to accept new thoughts and ideas. The hypothetical negative thoughts can be replaced by practical and realistic thoughts. The therapist plays an important role in calming the person and making the person more aware of the thought patterns and encouraging him to interpret differently and in a better manner.

Cognitive Behavioral therapy is based on the principle that out cognitions or thoughts are responsible for our behavior and not the external events. How a person reacts to a situation depends on his perception of the situation.

35

CHAPTER 2
HOW TO RETRAIN YOUR BRAIN AND DEAL WITH STRESS

If you are one of the forty million Americans who deal with an anxiety disorder, then you have no doubt experienced symptoms that you found unpleasant. The good news is that with proper treatment the majority of your anxiety symptoms can be deal with. The most successful clinical treatment for anxiety is called cognitive behavioral therapy or CBT. This book will examine the ways in which CBT can be useful for patients looking to take back their lives. Overcoming anxiety with cognitive behavioral therapy is not a difficult undertaking, but it will take time, dedication and a willingness to examine some of your key beliefs about yourself.

CBT works by requiring patients to think about the ways that they think about their anxiety. In nearly all cases anxiety is brought about and reinforced by a particular fear. In the case of social anxiety, this fear may be that a person will embarrass themselves or be seen in some way as defective. In the case of a phobia, the fear may be that the person will die in a plane crash or experience some other unwanted outcome.

CBT works by eliminating the thinking errors that go on between the patients ears. Often times they associate consequences with an action when the consequence does not logically follow from that action. For instance, in the case of the person with social anxiety, other people are not always thinking that they are incompetent after a social interaction. It is the belief in these consequences that causes the fear and the escalation in the anxiety.

By removing the association, it becomes possible for the patient to think logically about a situation without being overwhelmed with irrational fears. For this reason, research indicates that cognitive behavioral therapy works in about 90% of cases.

Cognitive behavior therapy has been used to help patients who are suffering from depression, anxieties, addictions and all sorts of other psycho social problems.

When undergoing cognitive behavior therapy a professional helps the suffering person to readjust his or her thinking. It is believed that thinking patterns and the way a person may perceive or relate to certain situations are connected with the patient's emotions and behavior.

Cognitive behavior therapy is a way to help find the

underlying causes of the problem from a psychological point of view and then change or correct the thinking pattern that has led to wrong behavior.

Using cognitive behavior therapy, a professional is trying to modify the unrealistic and distorted thinking of the patient. This in turn will help the patient to make changes in behavior and to be able to re-adjust. Thinking patterns and emotions play a key role in human behavior and can be changed or modified.

Cognitive behavior therapy is also used to help people with drug addictions such as cocaine. In the strictest sense of the word, people who turn to drugs, both legal prescription drugs that are addicting, as well as illegal drugs, can be said to have a behavior disorder and can benefit from cognitive behavior therapy.

There are an increasing number of people who are suffering from dysfunctional disorders and while some believe medical treatments may be enough. studies seem to indicate that cognitive behavior therapy is successful. Of course, a lot depends on the person's willingness to comply with a trained therapist and to modify inner thoughts and feelings.

The trained therapist also is helping the patient to understand past experiences and situations, to analyze and to learn not to react in an irrational or distorted way.

Cognitive behavior therapy has become a way of understanding the connection between inner thoughts and perceptions and human behavior. This no doubt has contributed to some success that has been made. It also has helped some people to make big changes in their life.

If you are a person who is suffering from anxiety or depression or any other kind of psycho-social problem, take courage and find a trained therapist in cognitive behavior therapy. You can learn to make changes in your life and help yourself and those who are close to you. Of course it may take you some time to see a difference in your life, but remember to accomplish anything worthwhile you need determination.

The time you may spend can make the difference. The good news is that, even if you feel overwhelmed and discouraged at times, there is help for you. There is also help in form of seminars that you can attend to learn more about cognitive behavior therapy and how it can help you. Taking time to look over the information available may be your very first step to recovery. Learn more about the basic principles that underlie these kinds of treatments.

You may have heard, "Use it or lose it."

What you may not have heard, but will in years to come based on latest brain science, is "Train it and get more of it."

Mental or brain training goes beyond simple mental activity. It is the structured use of mental exercises or techniques aimed at improving specific brain functions, physically strengthening the brain areas you are training (they get more neurons and stronger connections among neurons). Over the last 10 years scientists have found that mental training can work if you use any of these four methodologies: meditation, biofeedback, cognitive therapy, cognitive training.

1)Meditation has been shown to improve specific cognitive functions such as attention. As such it can be considered as a brain training technique. A number of studies have compared people who practice meditation to people who do not. The problem with these studies is that people in both groups can be very different. Thus the benefits observed in the group practicing meditation could be due to other things. Recently, a more controlled study was conducted that showed a specific effect of meditation on attention, one of the main brain functions.

Styles of meditation differ. Some technique use concentration meditation, mantra, mindfulness meditation, while others rely on body relaxation, breathing practice and mental imagery. It is not known so far what aspects of meditation or which techniques are the best to train one's brain. Scientists are researching what elements of meditation may help manage stress and improve memory. Preliminary results in terms of the impact on brain functions seem promising.

2)Biofeedback-based devices measure and graphically display various physiological variables such as skin conductivity and heart rate variability, so that users can learn to self-adjust. It has been used for decades in medicine. Recently, this technology has emerged in reasonably-priced applications for consumers who want to learn how to manage stress better. Neurofeedback is a subset of biofeedback relying specifically on electrophysiological measures of brain activity. Using Electroencephalography (EEG) biofeedback to measure brain waves gives the user feedback on different "mental states" like alertness. Neurofeedback is still a tool mostly useful in research and highly specialized clinical contexts.

3)Cognitive Behavioral Therapy (CBT) is based on the idea that the way people perceive their experience influences their behaviors and emotions. The therapist teaches the patient cognitive and behavioral skills to modify his or her dysfunctional thinking and actions. CBT aims at improving specific traits, behaviors, or cognitive skills, such as planning and flexibility, which are executive functions, depression, obsessive-compulsive disorders, and phobias. It has been shown effective in many studies and contexts such as depression, high levels of anxiety, insomnia. Doctors used CT to help dieters acquire new skills in order to achieve their goals.

4)Cognitive training: the new kid on the block

For many years, neuropsychologists have helped individuals suffering from traumatic brain injuries relearn how to talk, walk or make decisions, etc. Among other tools, cognitive exercises (including computer-assisted strategies) have been used to retrain abilities. However these tools are not available to the public and not everybody can afford a neuropsychologist or needs to see one. Things are changing as a variety of commercial programs is now making brain training available to the public. The challenge is to make informed decisions on which tools may be appropriate for your specific needs and goals.

How do I know what will work for me?

To determine if something works we first need to define what we mean by "work". A machine to train abdominal muscles probably won't "work" if what we measure is blood pressure. In the same way, a program training auditory processing speed may not work if visual functions are measured. This is why to determine whether a brain training software "works" it is crucial to (a) understand the claims made by the developer as to what abilities are trained, (b) find well conducted scientific studies showing that these abilities are indeed trained by the program and (c) decide whether that training is relevant to one's needs and objectives.

Another important aspect when evaluating whether a brain training program "works" is to look at the extend to which the training effects transfer to untrained tasks. It is well established that practice usually triggers improvement in the practiced tasks. So the first requirement for a well working brain training program is to show that people who use the program get better at the tasks trained. The second and more important requirement is to show that this improvement transfers to other, untrained, tasks, mostly tasks performed during everyday life. This would show that the cognitive and self-regulation abilities targeted by the program were indeed trained.

These are the mental abilities you can build using the different methods discussed above:

1) Meditation: attention, stress management

2) Biofeedback: attention, stress management

3) Cognitive therapy: self-regulation, especially when facing anxiety or depression

4) Cognitive training: working memory, speed-of-processing, auditory processing

Isn't it amazing how difficult it can be for any of us to change a bad habit or behavior? It can be a habit that is very simple such as losing your temper behind the wheel of a car or a more challenging one such as trying to break a serious addiction to say, smoking or over eating. Whichever it may be, it's important for you to know that you're not alone.

One reason why change can be so difficult is because we have engaged in the habit or behavior for so long, it has become second nature. It's almost like we're on "automatic pilot." As a result, we just engage in the behavior without thinking that we have a choice to do something different in the moment. We forget that we're blessed with a free will to choose.

Our emotions have a powerful effect on our body, giving it all sorts of stress related illnesses.

Our mind creates our emotions. What we think is happening is the beginning of our emotional responses. Emotions begin with an event that we interpret, thus all emotions begin with the thoughts that are our interpretation and opinions based on our automatic habitual responses to certain events.

We all know that everyone responds at times inappropriately to a situation because they have misinterpreted it. Sometimes it is so clear we cannot comprehend how anyone could have gotten it so wrong. The reason is the automatic habitual responses which are not emotional. Habits are intellectual because we have to learn something by repeating it enough times and train our mind to respond in that way.

We spend the second half of our lives ruled by the habits we formed in the first half.

If we want to change our automatic responses, we need to change our fixed opinions which are the foundation of our habitual responses.

Teach a child that if someone says they like you, that means they like you. And if someone says bad things about you, that also means they like you. That child will never be upset or hurt by anyone. Sadly we are not taught that, even though we know it is often true.

When young boys and girls tease each other, that is because they like each other. When adults put other people down, usually it is because they are jealous, and thus admire the other person.

What we must do is start to see the hidden reality of what people are really saying and feeling, and then you will have a different reaction.

Begin with the desire to change your habitual responses to always seeing everything as positive, that you will see everything in positive light as funny or a joke. Eventually you form the habit of never getting insulted or hurt by anything anyone says to or about you. It is a matter of choosing your habitual response and forming that new habit.

We really are nothing more than trained dogs. If you accept this objective truth, you can become your own master and teach yourself new tricks.

We can think our body into health or illness, but the intellect that thinks is a much slower and less guaranteed effect than the power our emotions have over our body. Thus repeating words is not going to do anything, but feelings can have very quick effects.

If you want to change your physical health, for better or worse, you must do it through emotions. As i said previously, our emotions are a product of our intellect. By changing our automatic habitual responses to those things which currently upset or stress us, we will have the power to change our health and life.

Based on the research that's been conducted over the last twenty years on the brain, we now know much more about how the brain works. The benefit to this information is that we can begin to understand why we often do the things we do in regard to behavior and actions in our lives.

Various studies have shown that our conscious mind is only responsible for 2 - 4% of our thought patterns and behavior. This is why when we use will power and persistence to overcome a bad habit or change a behavior, we usually have sub-par results. Short term the action or result may change but if we want to realize lasting change in our life, we must start at the beginning of the cycle, which is thought and behavior.

Recent brain research has shown that the subconscious or implicit memory system is responsible for up to 96% of our thought patterns and behavior. Based on the mechanics of the mind, if we really want to illicit change in our life, this is where we need to focus. As these studies are fairly new, just learning how to change our approach to habit and behavior is a re-learning experience in itself.

We begin to develop brain connections at a very early age, say five years old or so. When we develop brain connections, we are also creating what is referred to as cellular connections. Over time and repetition, the brain and cellular connections actually leave a foot print on our neural network in the brain. They become fixed in our subconscious and wha-la, we have developed a habit or behavioral pattern.

All success and happiness begins with your thoughts based on where you think you want to be in life. Your present circumstances will always control your thoughts and behavior based on your perception of reality, unless you're consciously aware of you're behavior. Studies indicate that all results are effects or a function of what we're thinking, feeling or doing based on our past.

So, what can we do to change our thought patterns and behavior?To change your thought patterns and behavior, you first need to recondition the thought patterns of your past. This is the key to realizing long lasting change. Because thought impacts emotions, what you end up feeling loops back to what you're thinking. As a result, you continue to repeat the behavior or action, which is why you end up with the same results based on your present circumstances.

It's a vicious circle but it doesn't always feel like one because we've become comfortable with the behavior. Over time we actually begin to accept that it's who we are. Believe it or not, we can experience joy from a negative or painful behavior based on our personal association with the behavior. If the behavior feels familiar, we become comfortable with it, so we think it's good for us.

We feel secure and in control because it's a familiar emotion.

Your subconscious, which represents your interpretation of past events,is responsible for your perceptions, feelings and behavior in the present. I refer to these as The Big 3. To change the Big 3, we must change our self-image, habits and beliefs, The New 3. This is where you ReTrain the Brain!

Essentially, what you need to do is create a release program in your brain, which will allow you to recreate your self-image. To create a new self-image, we first need to create new patterns of thought and behavior. This can be achieved by experiencing new affirmations, as well as visualization or meditation. These new affirmations and visualizations need to be created with emotion. They need to become more real than your present circumstances in order for the new affirmations to over ride or recondition your thought patterns and behavior.

Emotional Habits and CBT

It is commonly said that human beings are creatures of habit.

Usually, this characterization is used in reference to our behavior-though we've realized in recent years that how we think is also habitual. Since we all know that how we think has much to do with how we feel, a valuable question to ask ourselves is, What are my emotional habits?

What are emotional habits?

There are two dimensions to emotional habits:

How we generally feel, day to day, as we go about the business of living our lives.

How we emotionally react (over and over again) to specific situations/events that occur in our lives.

Thoughts and emotions cannot be separated; they are happening in tandem during virtually every moment of life. In other words, to be human is to be in a state of continuous thinking and feeling-and the subtle dynamics of that ongoing subjective experience are, in part, habitual.

The habits of anxiety, depression, anger, irritability, helplessness, sadness, jealousy, fear, worry, etc.

If we find ourselves repeatedly feeling worried and obsessive about what others think of us, or fearful about what our future holds, or depressed and jealous about how our lives compare to others'-it can be said that we've habituated ourselves into these repeating patterns.

This is not to 'blame' ourselves or to minimize the

impact of real events and situations in our lives. My point is to put us in the driver's seat and say that if we've habituated ourselves into these patterns, it follows that we can re-habituate ourselves out of them and into other/healthier patterns.

Beware of oversimplifying CBT (cognitive behavioral therapy)

CBT is of enormous benefit to individuals all over the world, and to the mental health field in general. However, the oversimplified statement (as it is appears in media sound-bites) that you can change your thinking and change your life can distort the true substance and value of CBT and the related methods of psychotherapy it has inspired.

Why?

Because it implies that changing your thinking is a simple and easy thing (like changing your shampoo or something). Also, it can lead one to the false belief that once you 'change your thinking,' the job is done. This couldn't be further from the truth. Becoming change agents with respect to our own habits of thinking and feeling is akin to learning and mastering a musical instrument, which I'll speak to a minute.

First, one more point about the potential to oversimplify CBT. Let's look at this often heard idea:

What matters most is not what happens to us, but how we respond to what happens to us.

I couldn't agree more. However, it is important that we take it a step further and clarify that our INITIAL response/reaction to 'things' is not nearly as important as how we respond over time-over the course of the hour, day, week, month and year.

In the moment we might blow up, shut down, freak out, minimize, not care, fall apart, have a panic attack, etc. Ok, fine, but THEN what do we do? And THEN...what do we do after that? And so on.

My point is that what matters most are not the discrete moments but the ongoing (and always imperfect) process of endeavoring to live well. In pursuit of this, it is helpful if we ask ourselves:

Is my basic orientation towards life centered around continuously seeking to learn and grow from life's challenges and complexities?

-or-

Am I living a more reactive life that involves blaming others, avoiding responsibility and regularly complaining

that things are not as I would like them to be?

changing habits of thought & emotion is like learning to play the guitar

How to Master Your Emotions For Personal Grow

Mastering your emotions is just one component of personal growth, yet it is important for all other areas too. I will introduce a couple of ways you can start to master your emotions right away.

Awareness is important. By being aware, you'll realize at what point you negative emotions start to creep up or even explode. Most of the time you may be going about your day and not realize what is going on around you, much less what is going on in your mind. In Eastern psychology, awareness training is important for all areas of growth. And it is a key for emotional growth.

By training yourself to be more aware of what is going on inside and outside of you, you'll have a better command on your emotions (and be happier too). From being aware, you'll also find out what triggers are being activated to leads to any negative emotions you may have.

Triggers (or anchors) are a part of everything we do. They can be positive or negative. Each of our five senses can be used as a trigger. What thoughts come to your mind when you imagine the smell of a hot apple pie? The smell of a hot apple pie is an olfactory (sense of smell) trigger. Each person will react differently when exposed to certain triggers. What may be positive for one person may be negative for another. If the hot apple pie brings about a pleasant memory of being at home with mom to you, then another person may have a negative memory of an argument with mom.

The most important thing is to realize what trigger leads up to bringing about the emotional memory. If it is a negative emotion that is triggered, then either eliminate the trigger or change the perception of it. Meaning is only what you give each event and the trigger that releases the emotion. You have the ability to change the meaning of an event which will change the meaning of the trigger.

By being aware of your triggers and the emotions attached to each one, you'll go a long way to mastering your emotions.

Becoming someone who can play the guitar (which I do) is lifelong learning, and I think most would agree that it is ideally pursued as a labor of love. To my mind, the same is true for learning to change our thinking and our emotional habits.

It might seem difficult to cure panic attack, but there are several ways to treat it so that attacks are much less likely to occur. There is no known cause for this disorder, but there are a few factors that are believed to contribute to it. Stress and genetics have been associated with panic attacks. There's not much you can do about genetics, but there are plenty of ways to change how you respond to stress.

The other main factor involves how your brain reacts in situations that make you tense or anxious. Instead of having a rational response, your brain causes your body to go into the "fight or flight" mode. This defensive reaction leads to panic attack symptoms such as increased heart rate, troubled breathing, chest pain, and faintness. Changing how your brain responds is trickier than learning how to handle stress, but it can be accomplished.

In order to retrain your brain, psychotherapy is usually suggested as a cure for panic attack. Cognitive behavioral therapy helps you develop new thought patterns to replace the ones that lead to attacks in the first place. If a certain situation causes you to become anxious, this type of therapy will have you redirect your thoughts to something you consider non-threatening or pleasant in order to fend off an attack. By doing this, you are associating these new, positive images with the stressful situation instead of focusing on the negative image that causes you to panic.

The main advantage to this form of treatment is that you can learn to recognize what makes you nervous or anxious so that you're better able to deal with these situations. Therapy will also show you how to cope with this anxiety if you have trouble getting rid of it altogether. Knowing that you will have the ability to face your fears and respond to them calmly can give you that much needed boost of confidence you need to prevent panic attacks.

How you handle stress can be a big indicator of whether or not you are likely to suffer from an attack. Arming yourself with techniques to combat stress and anxiety might not cure panic attack for good, but it can help you prevent attacks. There are a variety of stress management methods that teach you how to cope with anxiety while remaining calm and centered. By focusing on these methods, you can distract your brain from reacting irrationally to stress. Yoga, meditation, deep breathing, and guided imagery are some of the techniques that you can use to accomplish this.

Dealing with stress is a good way to reduce anxiety and lessen your chances of having panic attacks, while teaching your brain to respond differently in certain situations is an effective way to cure panic attack. If you don't have the time and money to spend on therapy sessions, then fortunately there are home remedies that can help you achieve this cure. They work much more quickly and efficiently and will enable you to live calmly and happily without having to worry about having panic attacks

CHAPTER 3

WHAT IS SOCIAL ANXIETY?

Social anxiety disorder, also known as social phobia, is a psychological condition marked by excessive and irrational fear and avoidance of social situations. It is often wrongly confused with shyness, which is simply a lack of confidence in meeting new people, and is quite normal in people with a more diffident personality -- in fact, most shy people can function quite well in society. Social phobia, on the other hand, can be crippling, and in some cases can prevent sufferers from living a normal life.

Social anxiety disorder can sometimes affect people in a general way, making them intensely anxious and fearful of any situation where they come into contact with people. More commonly, however, it is triggered by particular situations which may be specific to the individual. These could include being the center of attention, eating or drinking in company, attending a party or social gathering, asking a question or giving a report in a meeting, or even using a public toilet.

Social Anxiety Symptoms

If you are a sufferer from social anxiety, and you encounter one of these situations, you will experience a number of symptoms which will clearly distinguish the condition from ordinary shyness or lack of confidence.

Psychological or emotional symptoms include being convinced that you are going to behave in an embarrassing or humiliating way, and being terrified that other people will see that you are in a nervous state. You may have an urge to escape from the situation, so overwhelming that you actually act on it.

Along with these psychological symptoms, you are likely to have physical symptoms, including palpitations or a rapid heartbeat, difficulty in catching your breath, sweating, and a feeling of dizziness or light-headedness. You could even experience nausea, upset stomach or diarrhea. These symptoms could amount to a full-blown panic attack, in which you can't breathe and may be convinced you are having a heart attack.

There are also a number of longer-term signs that you could be suffering from social anxiety. You may find that you regularly experience several weeks of intense anxiety, including difficulty in eating or sleeping, in advance of any social event, or an occasion where you will have to speak in front of a group. Possibly you will find you are unable to go anywhere on your own and always have to bring a friend with you, or that you regularly need to drink alcohol before a social occasion.

You can also take the well-known Social Anxiety Test, The Liebowitz Social Anxiety Scale to have a more precise determination on whether you are suffering from social anxiety disorder.

Why Do you Get it?

Social anxiety disorder is the second most common mental health condition in the USA, affecting around 19 million people, and twice as many women as men. It most commonly develops in the teenage years or young adulthood, although it can occur at any age, including childhood. Typical sufferers are people with very few, if any, social or romantic relationships, who tend to feel they are social failures or rejected by society.

As far as is known, there is no one single cause of social anxiety disorder, but research suggests it is likely to be due to a combination of psychological and biological factors. A large proportion of affected people can identify a specific incident in their past that caused them embarrassment or humiliation, and consider their phobia dates from this time. However, others say they have had the disorder since they were children and can't remember a time when they didn't have it.

Generally, subconscious responses of panic, fear and anxiety are controlled by the amygdala, two small organs in the brain that are part of the limbic system which regulates our emotional life. It's the amygdala that generate our immediate responses to fear-inducing situations, and normally keep them within reasonable limits. However, by being frequently exposed to anxiety-provoking stimuli, it is thought that the amygdala can be conditioned to respond with a higher than normal anxiety level, which makes people more prone to disorders such as social phobia.

How to Overcome Social Anxiety?

Social fear is tough to figure out and can be just as hard to overcome, but if you are able to find the root cause of your social fear you will have a much greater chance of overcoming your social phobia once and for all. This chapter will help you in your path to regaining your life...

Don't believe all that you read and hear

Often when a person suffers from social anxiety, they

will seek advice and help from friends, family and many will defer to the internet for advice on how to overcome social anxiety.

The problem with this method is that many of the people you will be seeking advice from have never experienced social phobia themselves and cannot relate to what you are going through. The internet is a great place to find information on gaining control over your social fears but there is a lot of bad information out there so you will need to sift through and find what works and what does not.

So many books would have written same rehashed information on how you can overcome social fear, but most are written by people who have never suffered that overwhelming fear of social situations that you are experiencing.

How You Got Social Anxiety

There is no one known specific cause for social anxiety disorder, however many medical researchers feel that there are three main causes including physical, biological and environmental factors.

Physical - social fear may have been triggered from an embarrassing moment from your past.

Biological - social phobia may be the result of a chemical imbalance with your serotonin levels

Environmental factors - occurs when you witness someone else having a humiliating social moment and you fear the same thing happening to you.

Signs of Social Anxiety

While there are many signs that you may be suffering from the effects of social phobia, many people often do not realize that these symptoms are signs that they are suffering from a mental illness and never seek treatment. The most common symptoms are:

Avoiding social situations due to fear of being made fun of, judged, embarrassed or humiliated

Increased anxiety or nervousness when in social environments

Physical symptoms such as sweating, blushing, upset stomach, confusion, pounding heart, shortness of breath, and even diarrhea.

Social Anxiety Treatments

There are three main types of treatment for social phobia, with the proper treatment you can overcome your social fear and live a happy and healthy life, but often times people waste a lot of time in overcoming their social anxiety due to listening to bad advice and suggestions from others who have no experience in dealing with social fear and are merely offering their opinions.

The key with any good social anxiety treatment plan is to reprogram your brain in how it processes your thoughts, feelings, habits, and behaviors.

I know this seems like a lot but really with the right training and a sound plan of attack, overcoming social anxiety is really a lot more attainable and manageable than many people make it out to be.

Here are the three main types of social phobia treatments available:

Cognitive-Behavior Therapy - looking into your mind and your thoughts and how they affect how you feel in social situations. Once you have reprogrammed your thoughts and feelings you can really start the process of overcoming social anxiety.

Medication- anti-depressants, anti-anxiety and beta blockers are sometimes used in combination with cognitive-behavior therapy to reduce your anxiety levels but anxiety medication will not eliminate your social anxiety long term and once you stop taking them your anxiety returns. There are also many ill side-effects that have been reported with these types of medications.

Neuro-linguistic Programming - is among the most power forms of social anxiety treatments available. You are finding your personal power buried deep inside and getting to the root causes of your anxiety.

It is possible to treat social anxiety disorder with medications, such as antidepressants or sedatives. However, this is not considered the best way to go, as it helps to alleviate the symptoms, but doesn't get to the root of the problem. On the other hand, there are a variety of therapies which have proved very effective for large numbers of people.

One of those most widely used for social anxiety is CBT or cognitive behavioral therapy. This is a talking therapy that aims to help you change the way you think and behave. It is based on the idea that your emotions, thoughts, physical sensations and actions are all interconnected and affect each other, so that negative thought patterns can cause you to be trapped in a vicious cycle -- these patterns can be changed by helping you break down your problems into manageable segments.

A particular type of CBT that is often used with social anxiety is exposure therapy. Because simply talking about feelings is sometimes not enough, exposure therapy trains you to deal with actual situations, initially by imagining the situation, and working through your fears in a non-threatening environment. You can then be gradually exposed to the real-life situation, with the therapist's support.

A very specialized form of CBT is The Linden Method, which focuses on the changes that take place in the amygdala in the brain, to give rise to social anxiety. The idea is that as the amygdala have been conditioned to produce these extreme responses in your subconscious mind, your subconscious needs to be retrained to respond appropriately. The method offers 9 pillars, or guiding mantras, for you to follow, and complying with these on a regular basis can help you overcome and eliminate your anxiety. Many people say they have found this very effective for treating social anxiety.

There is no way of actually preventing social anxiety disorder. However, the sooner you seek help after your symptoms become apparent, the more effective your treatment is likely to be. With treatment, the outcome is usually very good, and many people go on to live happy and productive lives.

COGNITIVE BEHAVIORAL THERAPY A SOLUTION TO SOCIAL ANXIETY

What would you think if I told you that your anxiety wasn't the true problem, but the true problem you have is the way you hold onto, and battle with your social anxiety disorder. When we put great effort into trying to 'push away' our issues related to fear, that is the very moment it becomes chronic. When it comes to social anxiety many people tend to turn to one or more of the 4 'solutions' that we may be told will help our suffering, these solutions are:

1) Cognitive Behavioral Therapy: In my personal experience I still believe CBT is the fastest way to see results when it comes to overcoming social anxiety. This is because of 2 reasons, #1) Because it gets to the root of the problem which is that our thoughts create our feelings and ultimately the way we behave, #2) It makes you do homework when you're not in delicate situations and this creates better understanding and confidence when faced with an uneasy situation.

2) Herbs, Vitamins and Other Natural Treatments: With the endless amount of things to take for your social anxiety out there to accommodate your road to recovery, in my experience nothing beats a good vitamin B complex to help your nervous system fight the symptoms

of anxiety experienced due to prolonged sensitized nerves.

3) Drug Therapy: There is truly no way of knowing whether or not drug therapy will work for you. Popular ones such as Paxil and Zoloft have given sufferers relief from symptoms of anxiety, but in my experience working with people, solution #1 will always be the safer and more effective choice.

4) Doing Nothing: Many feel that their social anxiety disorder will go away if they just spend enough time doing nothing. Unfortunately I haven't seen a single case where this has worked. As we all know to accomplish anything in life you need something that drives you when you wake up in the morning. Similarly when you put in the effort to overcome pieces of your social anxiety. You begin putting yourself in those uncomfortable situations where you can challenge yourself, as well as use the techniques and knowledge that you learned as you begin chipping away and growing your confidence.

I can truly tell you that no person out there can save you from your fears, only you and your determination to not let social anxiety disorder run your life, can free you from the crippling fears you may be experiencing. The first step is always the scariest but also the most rewarding, the snowball effect one may feel after overcoming a fear related to their social anxiety will truly spread into other parts of their lives.

CHAPTER 4
OVERCOME ANXIETY WITH HYPNOSIS

Anxiety is a disorder that can negatively affect every aspect of a person's life. A person who experiences anxiety may become panicked if a certain situation occurs. For example an individual who has anxiety about financial matters may experience a panic attack, stress and extreme worry if their car needs to be repaired or something breaks in the house. Someone who experiences anxiety at work may be looked over for promotions and raises.

Anxiety is fear and worry that can take control of a person's life. An individual who has anxiety will learn to avoid certain situations that cause worry or panic. Some common anxieties are fear of social situations, fear of authority, fear of relationships and fear about money. There are dozens of anxieties that a person can have. Anxiety can lead to other mental disorders such as agoraphobia or obsessive compulsive disorder. Anxiety does not have to control one's life. There is an effective way to overcome anxiety for life.

Hypnosis is a proven method for overcoming anxiety. The process of hypnosis is rewarding, positive, safe and gentle. There are many benefits to undergoing hypnosis. A person who has undergone hypnosis will not only overcome anxiety but will have more confidence, increased self esteem and a more positive perspective on life. Hypnosis calms the nerves, the mind and the whole body while alleviating the stress and anxiety that an individual may experience. Hypnosis is an amazing process that dips into the resources of the subconscious mind.

When a person undergoes hypnosis that person is placed in a deep state of relaxation. As the state of relaxation progresses the subconscious mind becomes receptive to positive suggestions, new ideas and different perspectives. An individual in hypnosis will receive motivational encouragement, confidence building statements and a direct plan for overcoming anxiety. The beliefs, behaviors and thinking patterns of the individual will change.

Through hypnosis an individual can visualize themselves free from anxiety. The individual is able to "feel" how wonderful life is without anxiety. Life does not have to be full of anxieties but instead full of positive experiences.

Perhaps you don't remember an incident from your

past that triggers your anxiety. It doesn't matter. The important thing to know is that something happened and you made it mean "I'm not good enough" or "I'll never get it right" or "This is hard."

So self-hypnosis is simple. Here are the steps to take to overcome your anxiety:

1. Close your eyes and, as you breath in and out, say the word "relax" to yourself."

2. Imagine a situation in which you're anxious like taking a test or giving a speech. See yourself doing that activity. Be descriptive without adding any emotion or interpretation. For example, if you see yourself about to give a speech, simply see yourself standing in front of people. Visualize yourself, the room and the people in the audience.

3. Now say to yourself something like, " I'm powerful and dynamic." "Public speaking is easy and effortless." "I'm joyful when I speak to an audience." Keep repeating that phrase over and over. Do this for at least 5 minutes.

4. Open your eyes slowly and gently and return to wakefulness.

The key is to repeat that word or phrase over and over. That's how you self-hypnotized yourself into being anxious in the first place. You've hypnotized yourself so thoroughly that you no longer even notice that you're hypnotized. In a sense, you've hypnotized yourself through practice, practice and more practice.

So it will take repeated practice of replacing your negative self-talk with positive talk. In a sense, you'll be hypnotizing yourself from one hypnotic trance that produces anxiety to another hypnotic trance that serves you.

But you must keep practicing. In so doing, you're creating new connections in your brain that will produce new thoughts and feelings.

CHAPTER 5

HOW TO CURE ANXIETY THROUGH DEEP RELAXATION

Breathe Away Your Fears

Deep breathing from the diaphragm will add extra oxygen and allow you to bring that carbon dioxide level under control. This will ease the tingling and lightheaded sensations you may be familiar with. Deep and steady breathing is also very rhythmical and this can create a calming effect. Having the deep breathing technique to concentrate on also gives anxiety sufferers something on which to focus. Having something concrete and positive like "breathing techniques" can both distract and calm a nervous individual. How to overcome anxiety begins with mastering this one simple and very basic breathing technique.

Let Your Muscles Unwind and Relax

Being able to stretch and consciously relax the muscles in your entire body will relieve the tight, tense feelings, especially in the head and neck. Body muscles

74

will tighten in times of stress and panic as the body prepares to fight or flee the scene. With long periods of anxiety, the muscles become so tense that they will send pain signals to the brain. These symptoms translate to additional worry and anxiety, which then makes the muscles tighten up even more. Stepping the body down from its heightened state of tension with and alertness with relaxation and stretching can take some time and effort, but this is an excellent method to learn and use. This is another fundamental technique that shows you how to overcome anxiety on your own terms.

Stop the Worry Train in its Tracks

"Quit worrying", this is really great advice, and is probably the most powerful of all how to overcome anxiety techniques. However, this advice is much easier to give than it is to accept and put into practice. The best way to halt your worrying is by stopping it right in its tracks. You need to shut down those wandering, negative thoughts before they lead to those overwhelming sensations of stress, nervousness, and anxiety. With practice, you can learn to identify these feelings and thoughts at the very earliest stages. You can then consciously use positive thoughts and actions to defeat the negative anxious feelings. Just calmly talking to yourself and distracting your mind can help you "talk yourself back to normal".

Put Your How to Overcome Anxiety Techniques into Daily Action

How to overcome anxiety provoking thoughts and feelings can be accomplished by each individual. You just have to determine the way that is best suited to your needs and strengths. Once you begin to develop strong coping skills and relaxation techniques, you will discover that the negative, frightening feelings are occurring less frequently. As you make more progress in overcoming anxiety through self-control, you will find that the anxieties and thoughts that once controlled you are beginning to have less impact. Soon you will be back in control of your emotions and responses and will be emotionally stronger than ever.

There a lot of people who become overly concerned about various things in life and this often leads to anxiety disorders. In fact, this is a serious condition and many times it can aggravate to the stage where it leads to panic attacks. Panic attacks can truly disrupt your regular life and can make you feel as if you are going insane or dying and such disorders can increase your anxiety further than it was previously. Certain drugs are available to aid you in overcoming your anxiety and avoid panic attacks.

Pointers on controlling anxiety

You should start with trying to find out why you are experiencing higher level of stress. If you have just gone through a depressing ordeal such as a job loss or a divorce then it might be the cause of your anxiety. Therefore, you should learn how to control minor attacks so that if more severe attacks happen in the future it is easier for you to overcome them. You should try to figure out ways to control your anxiety in one step at a time when it is in the early stages. If a time comes when you are hit hard by anxiety attacks and it is becoming hard to overcome then a good idea for you would be to you visualize your self at the place about where you are having fears that a very dreadful thing might happen there. This way you can mentally go through the whole situation and then understand better that while it might be significant but it would most likely not have any lasting effects.

You can also try relaxation as means to control your anxiety and it is quite useful in doing so. You can use a number of relaxation methods to aid you by relaxing your mind and body in controlling your stress more effectively. For example when in stress try breathing more to vanquish your anxiety. Take deep and slow breaths through your diaphragm and breathe through your nose to induce relaxation.

It is also effective to learn to relax your body as well along with your mind. Focus on particular body muscles and relax them after flexing while lying in a straight position. You should also try some exercises to help you lose the adrenaline generated by your body and to relax you as well. You will also feel better after doing it. A substance known as endorphins is released when you exercise which not only helps you to feel good but also aids you in overcoming your stress more effectively by keeping you in a better frame of mind.

CHAPTER 6
HOW TO OVERCOME DEPRESSION THROUGH COGNITIVE BEHAVIOUR THERAPY, SELF-HYPNOSIS, AND DEEP RELAXATION

A very common habit among youngsters is to use the line, "I am depressed!", when they are simply sad or upset. People don't realize the enormity of the word depression and tend to use it as a substitute to sadness.

Most often we think that depression is just a case of extreme sadness. When we are faced with a tragedy, we feel depressed. But after a while it goes away. That's what the general belief is. But depression is far more than a mere bout of sadness. It is something with the potential to cause extreme harm and ruin lives, if not treated appropriately.

Keeping the magnitude in mind, let me throw some light on what exactly depression entails.

What is depression and why is it caused?

- Depression is a state of being where a person tends to feel absolutely empty, anxious and lost. It is the lowest point on the emotional scale and is marked by a variety of negative feelings like, guilt, helplessness, anger, irritability, etc.

- Depression is much more than an extreme mood swing. It is a behavioural disorder, which like any disorder needs treatment. No matter how happy a person may be, if there is depression, it needs to be treated.

- Depression is not to be confused with sadness. Sadness is an emotion. No doubt it is painful and negative, but it is nowhere as serious as depression.

- Depression can be caused due to a variety of reasons. Some of the most common ones include traumatic events from ones childhood, sexual abuse, family pressures, etc. Loss of a dear one can also be a reason.

- Some other reasons could include life changing events, like childbirth, menopause, any medical diagnosis, etc.

- Among adolescents, the highest number of depression cases are due to societal rejection, bullying, peer pressure etc.

- Certain medicines, like medication for Hepatitis C, sleep medication, high blood pressure medication, etc. are also known to cause depression. Such cases are known as medically induced depression.

- Another major cause for depression is substance abuse, narcotics, etc.

Types of depression

1. Major Depression: This is the most commonly known type of depression. It is also referred to as Major Depressive Disorder. It can be caused due to any major event or even a series of smaller events or problems. A person is diagnosed with major depression if he/she displays symptoms of depression (given below types) for over two weeks.

2. Persistent Depressive Disorder: If a person has undergone depression for over a period of 2 years, it is called persistent depressive disorder. Although the cause of depression may be same as major depression, for some reason the person may be incapable of overcoming it. Previously PDD was known as dysthymia.

3. Manic Depression: Manic depression is more commonly known as Bipolar Disorder. In the case of bipolar disorder, a person experiences extreme mood swings, ranging from unbelievable highs to depressive lows. The person cannot control his behaviour and may take drastic steps. Manic depression is one of the most serious forms of depression.

4. Seasonal Affective Disorder: It is a form of depression which is seasonal in nature, mostly happens during the winters. People, who have seasonal depression, find it difficult to cope in the lack of bright sunlight. Hence during winter, their depression peaks.

5. Psychotic Depression: People suffering from psychotic depression, have symptoms similar to depression along with psychotic symptoms like hallucinations, delusions, paranoia, etc.

6. Post-Partum Depression: This is the form of depression that women experience in the period immediately after childbirth. This could happen because of the obviously overwhelming experience, excess attention to the new born, etc.

The above given types are the 6 most common types of depression diagnosed among people. While the impact and the treatment for these forms of depression may differ, the symptoms are similar for most of them. Listed below are the most common symptoms.

Symptoms of Depression:

- Lack of appetite or excess of appetite.

- Lack of interest in activities you once loved doing.

- Sudden weight loss or weight gain

- Sleeplessness (insomnia) or excessive sleep

- Fatigue

- Reckless behaviour

- Thoughts of death, suicide, etc.

- Self-hate or self-loathing

- Unexplained guilt and anger

- Crying for no reason, getting upset easily

CHAPTER 7
COGNITIVE BEHAVIOR THERAPY TREATEMENT FOR DEPRESSION

Cognitive Behavioral Therapy (CBT) is a abbreviated form of psychological used in the direction of adults and children with natural depression. Its focusing is on prevalent issues and symptoms versus more traditional forms of therapy which tend to focus on someone's past yesteryear. The usual format is weekly therapy sessions coupled with daily praxis exercises designed to help the sufferer apply CBT skills in their home surroundings.

CBT for depression involves respective important features: identifying and correcting unfaithful thoughts associated with depressed sensitivity (cognitive restructuring), helping patients to pursue more often in gratifying activities (behavioural activation), and enhancing problem-solving skills. The first of these components, cognitive restructuring, involves cooperation between the patient and the expert to reckon and modify habitual errors in thinking that are associated with depression. Depressed patients often undergo contorted thoughts about themselves (e.g. I am stupid), their environment (e.g. My life is direful) and their prospective (e.g. There is no sensation in going forward, nothing will work out for me). Message from the patient's current experience, bygone history, and future prospects is used to counter these distorted thoughts. In addition to self-critical thoughts, patients with depression typically cut back on activities that have the possible to be enjoyable to them, because they expect that such activities will not be worth their exertion. Regrettably this usually results in a deplorable cycle, wherein dispirited mood leads to less activity, which in turn results in further depressed mood, etc.

The second portion of CBT Therapy, behavioral activation, seeks to remediation this downward spiral by negotiating increases in potentially satisfying activities with the patient. When patients are depressed, problems in daily realistic often seem unsurmountable. In the final, the CBT therapist provides and counsel in special strategies for solving problems (e.g. breaking problems down into small steps).

Cognitive Behavioral Therapy is a scientifically well-established and effective treatment for depression. Over 75% of patients show noteworthy improvements.

Cognitive behavior therapy has been around for quite some time and has in recent years become a very viable option in the treatment of depression. This type of treatment is not a quick fix for depression. It will require hard work on the part of the depressed person. This can be difficult because the nature of depression is that the person will not have any motivation to seek out therapy or deal with their problem. That is the depression controlling the situation.

Treating depression with cognitive behavior therapy will require the depressed individual to keep a diary of their feelings about the significant events in their life. The goal is to question and change the thoughts that the depressed person will experience through their depressed eyes. The goal of cognitive behavior therapy is to question and test the assumptions that are made about events in the patient's life. The treatment will seek to replace irrational thoughts with more helpful and realistic beliefs and assumptions.

This type of treatment for depression can be done on an individual basis or in groups. It has proven to be very successful in the treatment of depression, but the work is very difficult. The patient will have to want to change their way of thinking and behaviors. It can take a great deal of time for a patient to see results from their treatment. But once the healing has begun it is very profound.

For those who have been experiencing on and off throughout their life and have never sought this kind of treatment, it might be the treatment they have needed. Cognitive behavior therapy gets to the root of the cause of depression, which is a maladaptive thought pattern and behaviors. This approach is often a way for a depressed person to help their depression in a more permanent manner. Often drug therapy will help the person to feel better enough to work on their problems, but does not go far enough in treating the source of the depression.

Cognitive behavior therapy has provided many patients with relief from depression and anxiety as well as many mood disorders. It is worth looking into for the treatment of a difficult and long-term depression.

Psychologists use cognitive therapy to assist you in recognizing how the cognitive maladies or distortions make your life difficult. This therapy empowers you to govern your thoughts and therefore feelings. Its effectiveness can be as good as antidepressants if applied consistently and correctly. In some cases of chronic depression, it's extremely helpful to use a combination of antidepressants and cognitive therapy. The psychologists guide you to be conscious of your pessimistic thoughts and replace them with positive ones. This therapy can be imparted in both group settings and one-on-one basis.

Popping a pill can seem far easier than practicing this therapy, but in many cases it has been much more beneficial. In effect, its actually quite simple to apply, you just need to accustom yourself to cheerful thoughts by breaking away from the web of melancholic ones.

CHAPTER 8
SELF HYPNOSIS FOR
DEPRESSION

If you're depressed, self hypnosis may be the last thing on your mind. There again, a lot depends on the reason for your depression. If you recently lost a job, spouse, or are going through another sort of life change, depression might be a natural reaction to that.

It's not necessarily unhealthy. If, however, nothing has obviously changed and you've been depressed for a few weeks, that's something you might need to look at. Maybe you're the kind of person who has struggled with depression for most of your life. If this is the case, then self hypnosis can definitely help you.

Depression, you see, can be a learned behavior. As such, it can also be unlearned. If it was programmed inside you when you were very young, hypnosis is the ultimate tool to deprogram your subconscious mind and give you healthier tools to function. The very first thing you need to do is to accept that your depression is a temporary state. Even if you've been depressed for months, or even years.

The next thing to do would be to journal. Write down your very first experiences with depression, all the way up to the present time. Write down every thought, emotion, and action that surrounds your depression.

Why do this? What does this have to do with self-hypnosis?

By journaling, you're finding ammunition you can use while you're in a trance state. For example, after you've written a few pages about your depression, you might look back and find you've written a lot about anger. That could be a very powerful weapon once you're in a trance. When journaling, you naturally go into a semi trance state, and you might discover factors surrounding your depression that you would otherwise never touch on.

The next step is to get yourself into a trance. This is not as difficult as it seems. Sit or lie down, and start to notice your breathing. Don't try to control it; just notice it.

Then, imagine a feeling of relaxation beginning at your feet, working its way up the rest of your body. When your entire body is relaxed, slowly begin counting from 10 to 1. With each number, you relax deeper and deeper. At 1, you are totally at peace, completely relaxed. Then, find yourself in a scene. You might be on a beach, or in the mountains. This might be a place you've been before, or a place you'd like to someday visit, or it might be a place you've just made up.

Totally immerse yourself in this scene. Engage all of your senses. For example, if you're on a beach, really feel the sand under your feet. Hear the gulls overhead. Smell the breeze coming off the ocean. This kind of immersion deepens your trance.

Then, bring to mind your depression, or an emotion you've identified that's connected to your depression. Count again, this time from 3 to 1. When you get to 1, you'll be in a place in your past where you experienced this emotion.

Immediately look around you now. Is it day, or night? Are you indoors or outdoors? Are you alone or with somebody?

What's going on in this scene that's connected to your depression?

When you've identified that, rewind your mental tape and replay it, only this time, change it to where the negative emotion is not created. Preferably, create a positive emotion or feeling in its place. This kind of reframing with self-hypnosis will create a new memory that will override the previous negative one. Depending on your level of depression, you might need to do this kind of session several times in order to clean out all the cob webs.

Believe it or not, but depression is a treatable and manageable disease. Whilst perhaps there isn't any universal cure for it, using hypnosis for depression can help manage it in ways a lot greater than you might initially think or believe.

Let's take for example the symptoms of depression. You have less motivation to do things, you feel quite lethargic and just don't see a point, a reason or any ambition in doing things. This presents quite a problem as the less we do things, the less in touch we are with the world around us, the more we can become depressed and the further we delve into this troubling psychological state.

Thankfully however, hypnosis can be used to help treat, but not cure, depression. The way hypnosis works is by sending your mind into a subtle yet deep subconscious state. When you're in this state you're more open and prone to suggestion than you are normally. It's by manipulating this state of the subconscious, and placing suggestions that are more likely to make the symptoms of depression easier to handle, that you'll be able to help treat this state.

Of course hypnosis is not without its skeptics. Some people will claim that hypnosis essentially is just a placebo effect, that you will something to happen enough and it does. This is pretty much essentially what hypnosis is! It is about making your mind believe in something enough so that it becomes a reality, and if the results of such a thing can be demonstrated to cause so much benefit for so many people, then obviously the processes of hypnosis do work.

Give it enough time and using hypnosis for depression will do wonders for you. This psychological state that you enter into can effectively rid you of a number of ailments that you may have, and treating depression is definitely possible. Like with all things, patience is a necessity, and you'll need to willingly guide yourself into these deep, euphoric, relaxing and ultimately blissful states of calmness that your mind and body experience as a result of hypnosis. This calm is derived from the your mind finally being able to relax itself after thinking about things so much each and every day.

So don't worry, and don't feel depressed or stressed. Give self-hypnosis a go, and your depression may just surprisingly be minimized, and who knows, it may even go away. I'm not saying that you'll come across a depression cure, but I am saying that you will come across a way that you can easily manage it

When looking for ways to help stop depression, many

suffers need a lot of support. Many quit looking for a guide for depressive disorder but this mental health issue can be addressed in a number of ways. You can take anti-anxiety approaches and complement treatments and therapist with self-hypnosis.

Many people seek support through self-hypnosis for other conditions. Anxiety is a very common problem that requires guidance. Hypnosis effectively reduces stress and anxiety. This is important because depressive disorder and anxiety disorders are closely linked even though they arc remarkably different.

Anxiety and Depressive Disorder

Depressive disorder and anxiety are different conditions with their own unique symptoms. People who seek help for depression are facing feelings like hopelessness, deep sadness, anger, and despair. A person who has high levels of anxiety feels panic, fear, and overall anxiousness.

Depressed people often find regular tasks completely overwhelming. Fatigue interferes with the ability to concentrate and personal relationships suffer greatly due to the mood disorder. Anxiety can interfere with a person's ability to work or relate to others because the fear of panic is so poignant.

Even though these conditions are very different, they can be treated using the same interventions. For example, antidepressants treat depressive disorders and they can be used to treat anxiety as well. Behavior therapy is used to treat both conditions as well.

Cognitive and Behavioral Therapy

You may feel depressed or anxious because your body tells you that you are. Cognitive and behavior therapy work to help you think differently about situations and your emotional responses. Behavioral therapy addresses the specific behaviors you exhibit and cognitive therapy helps you retrain your mind.

Your behaviors are all forms of communication. You act according to your inner thoughts and beliefs in many instances. When you are depressed, you have a tendency to follow your low mood. Behaviorists suggest that you take steps to change your behavior to lift your mood.

Cognitive therapy complements this approach because it supports positive thought processes. You take a logical, objective stance on your mood and work toward creating thoughts that help elevate your frame of mind. The drawback to cognitive and behavioral approaches is that they can take an extraordinarily long time.

Relaxation Therapy

Relaxation is a great tool to help stop depression and anxiety. These techniques serve to help you control your body's responses to panic and sadness. As you relax, your body releases chemicals that help elevate mood and calm your thoughts.

How Self Hypnosis Can Help Stop Depression

Self-hypnosis is the ideal complement to relaxation, cognitive and behavioral therapy. This approach can also make medication work better as well. Hypnotic states are naturally relaxing. The session provides time for you to unwind and set all negative feelings aside.

Once you are relaxed, you are better able to take in the suggestions offered by the hypnotherapist. The suggestions include many of the same cognitive exercises you find in therapy. Your behavior is also addressed while you are in the relaxed state.

Since you are calm and at ease, your subconscious mind absorbs the suggestions and puts them into action automatically. This makes self-hypnosis the ideal augmentation to help stop depression.

Let Relaxation Dissolve Depression

Early awareness of our states of depressed moods when we may feel hopeless, helpless, lonely and afraid of the future is our first step to help ourselves if we wish to avoid taking medicinal drugs prescribed under medical treatment.

We need to have a brief period by ourselves to honestly assess what is wrong with us. This is easiest to do if we take pen and paper and jot down the factors as they come to mind. It may seem to be an elementary exercise but it has real value and offers us a degree of self-control.

Perhaps it is our lifestyle at fault, perhaps it is our attitude to life, maybe it is because we have been disappointed or hurt in some way, or that we have never patterned for ourselves a plan for our lives. But we may find that we never have thought that we are responsible for making a life plan or for having a recipe for our own happiness.

After you have written out some thoughts put down your pen and sit quietly for a few minutes. With the wise reminder that we should seek to change those things that are possible to change in our lives, and refrain from trying to change factors that are beyond our control, or none of our business, we begin to contemplate the present need for a more relaxed mental attitude and perspective.

If we can find that we can sit upright, close our eyes and remain still for some minutes in a patient attitude of just waiting, our thoughts, instead of being stimulated, will begin to slow down automatically. Gradually we begin to feel lighter of life's burdens. We feel more comfortable in our body and happier in our emotions. Our thoughts may for a period of time be blissfully still and peaceful. We get a taste of what it is to be free of the weight of depression. It is a great feeling! If we can accomplish this in a short time, it is possible to go further.

Then it is best to join a group under a specialist teacher who knows how to help you with various techniques for physical relaxation as well as simple meditation to help your mind. It is easy enough to learn. The most difficult part is in reminding yourself to practise so that gradually the unconscious bad habits and reactions melt away allowing a 'new' you to emerge - one that naturally feels more content, positive and self-confident.

Only by dissolving the previous old feelings, habits and mind states can we feel this freedom as we allow the natural flow of positive energies to replace the old.

We all have equal access to the natural interests, excitement and other gifts that life offers us. No more wasting of life time in unhappy moods. We have the power to make a change.

We hold the key to our own mental health and fitness.

So dissolve the past, take a deep breath, relax and start now!

CHAPTER 9

THE PSYCHOLOGY OF ANGER

Anger comes from the Latin word, angere, which means "to strangle." Anger strangles us on a number of different levels. It is the emotion which is probably the most familiar to the majority of us. A consistent finding in those who have low self-esteem, migraines, ulcers, heart attacks, substance abuse problems, troubled work and interpersonal relationships and frequent job loss is that they are unable to master their anger. Rather than controlling their anger, their anger controls them. While anger is not the sole cause of these problems, the constant appearance of anger in such individuals indicates that it is a prime factor in all of these problems.

Too much anger is toxic. Anger and hostility result in dis-ease of all types. It is physically arousing and has damaging physiological correlates, such as increased heart rate, more cortisol (a stress hormone) dumped into your system, muscle tension, headaches, decreased mental clarity and clogged arteries.

Anger signals the fact that something or someone has come between you and a desired goal of yours. It is a call to action. The goal may be as simple as trying to get home during rush hour. Yet, when another driver rudely cuts you off on the freeway, your anger rears its head.

The emotion anger is frequently confused with the actions you take while angry. This doesn't happen with fear. You don't confuse the emotion fear with the act of running away. However, anger is nearly always thought to be negative and destructive, despite the fact that anger itself is merely a feeling. Anger, in and of itself, if not acted upon, is instructive, not destructive. Anger can be a good thing. However, for anger to be positive, you must first learn to manage your emotions. Then you have a choice as to how to respond to anger's signal

Four Types of Anger

To alleviate some of this confusion around anger, allow me to better acquaint you with the various types of anger. There are at least four types of anger of which we know: anger directed at self, anger directed at others, disappointment, and constructive anger.

1. Anger at Self

The first type is anger directed inwardly at oneself. The anger sits inside and burns and festers. After enough anger has been turned inward, it eventually leads to inappropriate angry outbursts at undeserving and unsuspecting people. Studies show that most people turn 90% of their anger inwards at themselves. Most of this anger is an attempt to control and contain the frightening emotion of anger. Anger can lead us to rage-filled, uncontrollable behaviors. Rather than feel the anger, honoring the feeling, and releasing it, most of us bottle it up. This stuffed anger is toxic and leads to all sorts of negative health outcomes. It also leads to displaced anger where you get angry with the wrong person, at the wrong time, and to the wrong degree.

2. Anger at Other

A second type of anger is directed outward. This type of anger builds upon itself and can frequently lead to rage. This form of outward-directed anger is typically displaced onto the wrong person, at the wrong time and in the wrong manner.

Both of the first two types of anger are destructive. Destructive anger includes anger that is directed inward and never released and anger that is inappropriately directed outward at others. Anger directed at others may be inappropriate in terms of its target (Are you directing your anger at the right person?), its intensity (Is the degree of anger in keeping with the offense?), its timing (Is this the best time to make your anger known?), and the manner in which it is communicated (Is this the best way to communicate my anger?).

3. Disappointment

The third type of anger exists in tandem with sadness and most closely resembles disappointment. Disappointment usually involves a judgment that has not been met. Judgments cause trouble for everyone. Judgments usually involve an element of moral superiority, as if you know what is best for someone else. Stay away from judgments.

4. Constructive Anger

The final type of anger is the type used as a positive motivator to act to remove an obstacle that is preventing you from reaching a goal. This type of anger can be a constructive anger, that is, an anger that is quickly released and prompts you to act in a positive manner to remove the obstacle from your path.

Constructive anger actually provides you with a persistent attitude which enables you to push forward to solve a given problem. These four types of anger have been demonstrated via several methods - reports from subjects in scientific studies, physiological evidence, and behavioral data. When increasing your emotional awareness, part of the task is to learn the variety of subtle emotional differences within one family of emotion. The better equipped we are to make subtle differentiations within an emotion, such as anger, the better able you are to share with others the degree of feeling you are currently experiencing. With that in mind, let us turn to the bodily cues that anger provides us.

Physiological Cues of Anger

In order to stop the cycle of anger, you have to tune in to the early warning signs. So pay attention! When you begin to feel angry, blood flows to your hands and feet, making it easier to strike at your perceived enemy, your heart rate increases, a rush of adrenaline kicks in and your body prepares for forceful action. Anger causes a surge of chemicals (catecholamines) which creates a quick, one-time rush of energy to allow for one brief shot at physical action. Meanwhile, in the background, another batch of chemicals, including cortisol, is released through the adrenocortical branch into the nervous system that creates a backdrop of physical readiness. This emotional under-tone lasts much longer than the initial one-time surge and can last for days. This undertone keeps the brain in a special state of overarousal building a foundation on which reactions can occur with great speed.

Compassion as the Antidote to Anger

If you want to reduce your anger, think of the universe as compassionate and nurturing. As such it is designed to reward compassionate, nurturing behaviors in individuals. Compassion transcends both natural human sympathy and normal Christian concern, enabling one to sense in others a wide range of emotions and then provide a supportive foundation of caring. Compassion occurs when a person is moved by the suffering or distress of another, and by the desire to relieve it. Compassion is empathy, not sympathy. It is the identification with and the understanding of another's situation, feelings, and motives. This ability to put yourself in the other person's shoes serves as the perfect antidote to anger in which one perceives an obstruction to one's goals.

The goal is to understand the situation from the perspective of the other person. Often this involves interpreting the situation with a large degree of grace. For example, I am driving 75 miles per hour in the fast lane. A car comes up behind me doing 100 mph. The driver comes inches from my rear bumper in a desperate attempt to get me to move aside. At this point, my former interpretation was "That idiot! What does he think he's doing? I'm going 75! I'll show him." And then I let off the gas to slow down ever so slightly. My current interpretation is "He's probably trying to get to the emergency room. Perhaps there has been an accident." And I change lanes and let him by. No anger.

How we can use constructive forms of anger against destructive forms of anger to develop better emotional health...

Anger is a powerful emotion; it can create havoc in our personal and social relationships and can even sometimes lead to dangerous consequences. So why do we get angry? Is anger constructive in any way or purely destructive? Is it possible to control anger by understanding its deeper psychological causes? Maybe with a proper analysis of an emotion, we can control the emotion instead of allowing the emotion to control us.

Many things or events, of great importance or even of least importance can make us angry. If the computer suddenly crashes when you are working on something really important, you can get angry. Similarly if your business partner works against your wishes, that too gets you angry. In fact sometimes the emotions in us become so important that the external event itself that caused the anger somehow recede to the background. Yet anger can be both constructive and destructive.

Anger, best defined as a feeling of displeasure, irritation or hostility can have different dimensions with mild to violent responses. Anger management is an important issue as stress, anxiety, irritation are persistent in modern life. Anger being primarily manifested negatively and being directed against someone, it is a social response and have social consequences. Psychological theories consider anger as a response to pain. Thus when we feel a sort of pain or irritation or go through unpleasant feelings along with a realization of a potential threat, we tend to get angry. Thus in anger there are two factors - a feeling of pain or displeasure, followed by a feeling of threat. When a partner says or does something unpleasant, we get angry because we feel pain and we also feel that the situation might threaten or jeopardize the partnership. The need for certain uniformity in life is strong in all of us and whenever we sense a disruption in this 'structure of life' that we like to hold on to, we become aggressive and angry. A tool is 'supposed' to work, when it doesn't we get angry. A relationship is 'supposed' to work, when it doesn't we get angry. So anger is largely a reaction against disruption of our preconceptions/presuppositions, we crave stability and security in life.

Eastern Philosophy considers anger as a result of ignorance or human folly that is a consequence of worldly attachment. The argument is if we can let go of attachment towards the object of anger, we will fail to become angry. However the fact remains that attachment is a basic truth of life and whenever there is attachment to anything, there is also expectation and breaking down of this expectation leads to anger. Psychoanalysis would consider anger as a form of gratification of the aggressive impulses, so when there is frustration of sexual gratification, anger can result. In fact anger in the form of sadism has been extensively explained by psychoanalysts as a form of sexual gratification through aggression. Aggression could also be related to feelings of narcissism and ego and as manifestation of the threat to our sense of identity.

Considering the physiology of emotions, William James has provided a theory and an explanation of what is regarded as the flight-fight response or the body's automatic response to face or flee from real or perceived threats. However subtle phenomenological differences in different emotions are not always accounted for as we still do not have a complete theory for the science of consciousness that largely controls emotions. James' theory suggests that any emotion is a response to physiological changes in the body. There are controversies to this theory although the physiological changes in the body during anger are well documented.

During anger, the amygdala of the brain sends out signals, body muscles become tense, neurotransmitters and hormones are released in the brain that quickly lead to a state of arousal. Amygdala of the brain being responsible for perception of threats and dangers, hypothalamus of the brain responsible for perception of pain or irritation are activated during anger and we react without the mediation of the cortical or reasoning part of the brain. Strong emotions like anger can be as 'blind' as strong emotions of love as both of these represent a state of arousal when our brains are not in a normal chemical or physiological condition, so to speak.

Responses or reactions to anger are all that we are concerned about as we may not be able to control the emotion per see, but can control its manifestations. People have different levels of reactions to stimuli and some people react quickly and with intensity to certain things or events whereas some others may react slowly and may not show the same intensity. Some people break glasses or burn objects when angry; some others engage in verbal or physical abuse towards the object of anger or towards a substitute object whereas some others control and suffer depression with aggression turned inwards. Although some amount of display of anger is psychologically healthy as it can prevent feelings of hurt, depression or feelings of self-destruction, overreaction towards an object of anger can be destructive to both the individual who is angry and the object of anger. Anger being reciprocal and contagious can actually create anger in the object of anger as well and so the object reacts aggressively or becomes passive with no reaction despite strong feelings of displeasure and resentment.

This leads us to the discussion on anger as a constructive and destructive process and to anger management. Anger management is tapping out the constructive potential of anger. Aggressive impulses are necessary, they help us to stay competitive and become successful by striving and working hard. Without inner aggression, we will never achieve anything in life aggression provides the zeal and life force so anger in measured forms is always good and have a constructive effect. Despite this we have to learn how and where to draw the line considering the situation and the person we are angry with.

We should understand exactly at which point a fine line separates the constructive and the destructive phase of anger. Anger management is locating this line by using reason even during the most irritated state of mind. How do we do this? This is only possible by holding back feelings of threat or danger by developing a form of inner boldness. Thus here constructive aggressive impulses can be used against destructive ones. How do we use anger against anger to stop anger? Sounds like a pun. But in a situation when we stop feeling threatened by being brave, we will stop being angry.

Consider a person extremely angry with his colleagues because he feels threatened that he will lose his job or self-respect. In this situation the best he can do is to feel less threatened by being confident that no matter what happens, he will not lose his job. This inner confidence, a sort of subtle aggression, is the key to anger management. Thus the two parts of anger - pain and threat cause reactions in us, we cannot do much about pain but we can do something about feelings of threat. We can ignore or overcome the threat with greater confidence. The traditional relaxation techniques or meditation or even talks of wisdom to control anger may not always work during an aroused state because our reasoning part of the brain fails to work when we are angry. But relaxation will naturally result if we don't feel threatened, if we cut out the threat part of aggression and exercise our self-confidence. So I would suggest that anger management is not about trying to force relaxation of the mind during an aroused state which is next to impossible because our body does not permit that, but rather to develop the constructive aspects of aggression within us so that we are aggressive or bold enough to confront all threats without getting tensed or irritated. Only subtle aggression can control violent aggression. Anger management is thus about developing the subtle deep rooted constructive forms of aggression, the inner confidence to overcome all destructive aspects of the emotion so that we can lead emotionally healthy and successful lives.

CHAPTER 10
THOUGHTFUL WAYS TO DEAL WITH ANGER

---

nger is an immediate reaction to an obstacle. It is a strong negative emotion of displeasure, hostility or fury that might occur to anyone on any occasion. Anger generates other bad feelings such as fear, disgust, shame, irritability, outrage, hostility and even violence and the aggressive response it generates can harm you. Anger is a punishment to you for somebody's fault.

Anger changes the behavior pattern of the person as a result of changes in his emotional status. it is accompanied by physiological and biological changes. Actions resulting from anger often lead to undesirable physiological and health consequences, because the neurotransmitters/hormones (eg. adrenaline) released during anger intensify impulsive action and obscure rational thought processes. It may raise your heart rate, the blood pressure and may result in hot reactions. If you hold on to anger so long it will give you tense muscles, stress and unhappiness. Anger is a silent killer. According to Mark

Twain anger is an acid that can do more harm to the vessel in which it is stored than to anything on which it is poured.

Anger can lead to problems at home, at work and elsewhere. It spoils the quality of your life wherever you are. Anger can destroy your relationship with your spouse, colleagues and others. The degree of your anger, the manifestation of it and the length of you staying in anger, need skillful management to avoid further problems. We can be angry on the right grounds, against the right persons, in the right manner at the right moment for the right length of time. But remember not to cross those borderlines any time.

Dealing with anger is a difficult matter and requires a lot of skills. Expressing, suppressing and calming are the three ways of dealing with anger. The healthiest way is to express your feelings in an assertive - and not aggressive - manner. Suppressing your anger and then converting or re-directing it to other positive ways, is another way. This way of handling of anger can cause hypertension, high blood pressure or depression. You can defuse anger through diversion, distraction, humor or by talking about it, so as to calm you down. The third way is to force you to calm down inside, by controlling internal responses. You can be angry every day but learn not to show it so as to minimize the problems it may create, by any strategic manner. Culture does not allow one to show anger. If anger is not allowed to express, it stays in disguise. Anger built up over years can break even marriages.

The best way to manage anger is to reduce the intensity of your emotional feelings and the physiological arousal. You can ignore what has happened or to choose to shrug it off. When someone does something which you don't like, why do you react to it by resorting to anger? When you are caught with anger, you should deal with it tactfully by pausing for a moment and reflecting on the situation. Then you can skillfully respond to the person who triggered your anger without attacking him. You cannot avoid or change the people that enrage you. But the easier possibility is that you can control your reactions. The real cause of your anger is inside you and not on others. Those who get angry easily have low tolerance, physiologically or genetically. Easily angered people come from disruptive and chaotic families.

When you get angry, think whether that element of anger is inevitable. We can consciously train ourselves to tolerate frustration or irritation without getting angry too much. You can deal with anger by accepting things and events as they are and realizing that you cannot change all the situations or individuals that irritate you. If you are angry, admit it to yourself and avoid prolonging it. Prolonging anger can lead you to self-destruction or self-defeat. Do not stay back with anger so long. Think of ways to express it constructively. You can express your anger to anyone who triggered your anger directly or over phone or in writing. But ensure that your reaction is calm, assertive and not aggressive. Aggressive way may escalate your hurt feelings. As well, if you feel so angry, you can talk your reactions to yourself or to any another person or even to a pet to unburden yourself and to discharge the anger. Don't postpone this till when you have overcome the anger and are feeling good later. Physical ventilation or exertion can drain off your anger. Do exercise, sports or physical activity to reduce anger. Mediate regularly to overcome anger overload.

The positive aspect of anger is that it helps us to recognize something is wrong somewhere. But don't get angry on anything and everything. When you get angry, choose to let it off, take a few breaths, or countdown to ten, or analyse why you are upset. Realizing that you are caught with anger is the right way to begin to deal with it. All your anger is about something what has happened in the past or will happen in the future and not what is happening in the present moment. So if you can be in the present moment you cannot hold on to anger for long. So be in the present moment to avoid holding on to anger.

Physical exercises can relieve your anger.

Let us look at the Kids. They get angry anytime and manage it beautifully. When they are in anger, they express their feelings openly, directly and allow it to go. Within minutes, they can start laughing, playing and leaving the anger behind by choosing to 'live in the present moment'. Nurture the nature of a child to deal with anger.

Anger will affect the quality of your life and the productivity at work. If you don't do anything about managing your anger, it will cause problems to you, and others in the society in which you live. The best way to deal with anger is to understand the nuances of anger. Manage it skillfully and lead a happier life.

The first step in being able to learn effective anger management techniques is to recognize the situations that make you angry and your body's warning signs of anger.

List things that can trigger your anger

Make a list of the things that often set off your anger (for example, running late for work and getting stuck in a traffic jam, your teenager leaving not helping out around the house or a co-worker blaming you for something you didn't do). If you know ahead of time what makes you angry, you may be able to avoid these things or do something different when they happen.

Pay attention to the warning signs of anger in your body

Notice the things that happen to your body that tell you when you are getting angry (for example, a pounding heart, flushed face, sweating, tense jaw, tightness in your chest or gritting your teeth).The earlier you can recognize these warning signs of anger, the more successful you will probably be at calming yourself down before your anger gets out of control.

Find anger management techniques that work for you

There are a number of different ways of managing anger and some strategies will suit you better than others. Here's some simple ways to put an end to the vicious cycle of stress that anger can bring:

Control your thinking

When you're angry, your thinking can get exaggerated and irrational. Try replacing these kinds of thoughts with more useful, rational ones and you should find that this has an affect on the way you feel. For example, instead of telling yourself "I can't stand it, it's awful and everything's ruined," tell yourself "It's frustrating, and it's understandable that I'm upset about it, but it's not the end of the world and getting angry is not going to fix it." Psychologists call this type of thinking "self talk."

Develop a list of things to say to yourself before, during and after situations in which you may get angry. It is more helpful if these things focus on how you are managing the situation rather than what other people should be doing.

Before:

"I'll be able to handle this. It could be rough, but I have a plan."

"If I feel myself getting angry, I'll know what to do."

During:

"Stay calm, relax, and breathe easy."

"Stay calm, I'm okay, s/he's not attacking me personally."

"I can look and act calm."

After:

"I managed that well. I can do this. I'm getting better at this."

"I felt angry, but I didn't lose my cool."

Take time out

If you feel your anger getting out of control, take time out from a situation or an argument. Try stepping outside the room, or going for a walk. Before you go, remember to make a time to talk about the situation later when everyone involved has calmed down. During time out, plan how you are going to stay calm when your conversation resumes.

Use distraction

A familiar strategy for managing anger is to distract your mind from the situation that is making you angry. Try counting to ten, playing soothing music, talking to a good friend, or focusing on a simple task like polishing the car, doing the dishes, folding laundry or walking the dog.

Use relaxation techniques

Relaxation strategies can reduce the feelings of tension and stress in your body. Practice strategies such as taking long deep breaths and focusing on your breathing, or progressively working around your body and relaxing your muscles as you go.

Learn assertiveness skills

Assertiveness skills can be learnt through self-help books or by attending courses. These skills ensure that anger is channelled and expressed in clear and respectful ways. Being assertive means being clear with others about what your needs and wants are, feeling okay about asking for them, but respecting the other person's needs and concerns as well and being prepared to negotiate.

Avoid using words like "never" or "always" (for example, "You're always late!"), as these statements are usually inaccurate, make you feel as though your anger is justified, and don't leave much possibility for the problem to be solved.

Try to acknowledge what is making you angry

Acknowledge that a particular issue has made you angry by admitting it to yourself and others. Telling someone that you felt angry when they did or said something is more helpful than just acting out the anger.

Make sure you think about who you express your anger to, and take care that you aren't just dumping your anger on the people closest to you, or on people who are less powerful than you. For example, don't yell at your partner, children, or dog when you are really angry with your boss.

Sometimes it can help to write things down. What is happening in your life? How do you feel about the things that are happening? Writing about these topics can sometimes help give you some distance and perspective and help you understand your feelings. Work out some options for changing your situation.

Rehearsing anger management techniques

Use your imagination to practice anger management strategies. Imagine yourself in a situation that usually sets off your anger. Imagine how you could behave in that situation without getting angry. Think about a situation where you did get angry. Replay the situation in your mind and imagine resolving the situation without anger.

Try rehearsing some anger management strategies with a friend. Ask them to help you act out a situation where you get angry, so that you can practice other ways to think and behave. Practice saying things in an assertive way.

CHAPTER 11
COGNITIVE BEHAVIORAL THERAPY FOR ANGER PROBLEMS

The emotion (or "feeling") of anger is a complex combination of physical sensations, cognitions (or thoughts), and behaviours.

The physical sensations associated with anger are well known. A racing heart, feeling short of breath, a dry mouth, butterflies in the stomach, trembling limbs, feeling hot and flushed etc. These may sound familiar - they are very similar to the physical sensations that occur in anxiety. This is unsurprising - it is the same physiological mechanism that underlies both emotions. Anger is the "Fight" component of the "Fight or Flight" response to perceived danger.

The physical sensations of both anger and anxiety are driven by hormones released by the adrenal glands (small pockets of tissue situated above the kidneys). These adrenal glands secrete adrenalin into the blood which rapidly disperses around the body. It is adrenalin that acts on the body to prepare it to either fight or run away by increasing the heart ("racing heart") and breathing rate ("short of breath and dry mouth"), raising the blood pressure ("feeling hot and flushed"), tensing the muscles ("trembling limbs") etc.

Common thoughts associated with anger include "He can't say/do that to me!" or "It's not fair!"

Behavioural manifestations of anger include clenching the fists, grinding the jaw and invading another's personal space.

It is very important to realise that all these 3 components interact and feed-back to one another, causing either an increase or decrease in the feeling of anger. For instance, if you're angry and you let yourself behave angrily - shouting and screaming for instance - you're body will secrete more adrenalin, thus increasing further the sensations of anger.

Anger per se isn't a problem - it is an emotion that has benefits in certain situations. The "anger" seen in animals when they're threatened or fighting over territory or mating rights is clearly a survival strategy. A passive, mild-mannered tiger isn't likely to live very long!

Fortunately for most human beings we no longer have to physically fight to survive, eat or find a partner. This makes a lot of our anger redundant. However, the "Fight or Flight" response has developed in us (and most animals) over millions of years so we will continue to get angry for the foreseeable future. This can cause us and others around us problems.

I'm not suggesting that we try and eliminate anger from our lives, but if we think it's causing us or others problems, we can try to moderate it and make it less damaging. Ideally we can make it work for us rather than against us.

CBT approaches anger by focusing on the thought processes associated with anger. The theory is that since our thoughts are a fundamental component of anger (along with physical sensations and behaviours), if we can moderate these angry thoughts we can moderate the other two components as well via the feedback mechanism.

Often it is our thoughts - our interpretations of events - that trigger the anger response in the first place. If we can develop a more balanced and rational interpretation of the world around us, we can nip the anger response in the bud. A good example of this is our response to criticism. If we interpret all criticism as a spiteful attack on us as a person, then we will get angry. If we are able to adopt a more balanced, rational view of criticism, we may feel disappointed but we will avoid getting "hot under the collar". We may even be able to see that sometimes our critic is right!

Another technique to moderate our anger is too think more flexibly. We've all seen toddlers and young children throw tantrums - they can be apoplectic with rage! Often this seems to be a result of immature, inflexible thinking - young children like to have (and make up) rules that must never, absolutely never, be broken, either by themselves or (especially) by others. Oh, the scenes of horror witnessed at children's parties when a child has "broken" the rules of a game!

Unfortunately, many of us adults continue with inflexible, never-to-be-broken rules to life. This is a problem if you want to avoid screaming and rolling around on the ground whilst wearing a suit. Examples of adult rules are "No-one must ever be rude to me", "Life must not be unfair to me", and (my favourite) "Other people must drive as well and courteously as I do".

There are many problems with these rules. First and foremost of which is that they're not really "rules" at all - they're your preferences. There is no law against people being rude to you, or life being unfair, or people not letting you out at junctions. You'd prefer it were otherwise, but that's all it is - your preference. As it turns out, most people are usually polite and drive decently, and the world may not be totally unfair after all, but there will always be exceptions. You can't control these exceptions, and by having such rigid rules you're setting yourself up for a lot of anger in your life. Try thinking along the lines of "I prefer it when things go my way, but sometimes they won't and I can accept and deal with that".

This leads to another technique for moderating anger - moderating the language we use. I don't simply mean avoiding swearing etc, but something more subtle than that, relating to both the words we use internally and externally. Language is a powerful thing - after all, our thoughts are made up of words (we a few pictures thrown in) - and we can use it to our advantage. So if something we don't like has occurred - someone's bumped our car in the car park - we can choose how to frame this event in language. We can think "I'd like it if they hadn't done that, they might have been more careful, this will cause me some inconvenience and expense" OR we can think "He's done this deliberately! He was probably drunk! How can this happen, today of all days!" One way of thinking uses moderate terms, the other uses extremes. Same event but different thinking responses. It's clear which response is not only makes this hassle more bearable, but also leads naturally on to sorting the hassle with a minimum of fuss.

Thinking more flexibly also involves accepting people - including yourself - as fallible human beings, capable of making mistakes and doing wrong. And yet despite these faults, they (and you) still possess dignity and are worthy of respect. This also means that we will accept that other people can have differing opinions and views and, even if we don't agree with them, we're not going to make ourselves angry trying to make them admit that they're wrong! Also, we're not going to label others (or yourself) as "nasty" or "useless" or "selfish" etc on the basis of one or two events or conversations. Everyone can, and probably has, been all of these things (and others) at some time in their lives, and probably on more than one occasion! If you label someone then not only are you being wholly inaccurate about a complex and changing human being, but you are also likely to interpret anything they do in the future on the basis of that label. If a "nasty" person coughs whilst you're giving a talk then obviously they've done it deliberately to annoy you. Cue the anger response!

A final way to moderate anger makes use of the interactions between thoughts, sensations and behaviours in a slightly different way. Rather than focusing on the thinking processes, this technique encourages you to focus on your behaviour. By moderating your behaviour you will provide "negative feedback" (also called "inhibitory feedback") to the anger response system,

128

dampening down it's effects. So when you next feel very angry, rather than stomp around, shouting, shaking your fists and being intimidating, try taking slow deep breaths, relaxing your hands, talking at a normal volume and at a normal rate etc. This calm behaviour will send the message "Things are OK" back to your body, causing the secretion of adrenalin to tail off and stop, thereby reducing and eliminating the physical sensations of anger. Interestingly, behaving like you're calm also works on your thoughts. So calm, measured behaviour leads to a calm body and mind.

The main problem with human beings and anger is that, for most of us, anger is no longer very useful. In our modern lives we mostly confront irritations and inconveniences rather than an enemy tribe or voracious wild animal. It is no longer appropriate for us to go red in the face and want to smash the place up. Using the techniques detailed above can help us to moderate our anger.

I say "moderate" and not "eliminate". I think it is neither possible nor desirable to remove a fundamental emotion like anger from a human being. We need some level of anger to prompt us to act appropriately in situations where our interests are threatened. We may not be in physical danger, but getting angry can galvanise us to act when our bosses are giving us too great a workload or our government is curtailing our liberties.

CHAPTER 12

ANGER & HYPNOSIS-THE POWER OF THE MIND

Controlling Anger through Hypnosis

Now a day's psychology is such a profound and a successful field though human emotions. In the field of understanding in the human mind deserves a bounty of effort and man power. The two major emotions that humans tend to struggle cruelly are depression and anger. Several say that controlling anger and depression is related to the point of view of our life and others demand that drugs are required. Everyone has an opinion to this delicate subject, and all of them assume only their is correct.

Anger is "an emotional state that varies in intensity from mild irritation to intense fury and rage," according to psychologist doctors. Anger is a completely normal, usually healthy, human emotion but it can stiffle our emotional freedom. But when it gets out of control and turns destructive, it can lead to problems-problems at work, in your personal relationships, and in the overall quality of your life. And it can make you feel as though you're at the mercy of an unpredictable and powerful emotion.

In dealing with anger, since it is impossible to fulfill all our desires or to stop unwanted things happening to us, we need to find a different way of relating to frustrated desires and unwanted occurrences. We need to learn patient acceptance. Patience is a mind that is able to accept, fully and happily, whatever occurs. It is much more than just gritting our teeth and putting up with things. Being patient means to welcome wholeheartedly whatever arises, having given up the idea that things should be other than what they are. It is always possible to be patient; there is no situation so bad that it cannot be accepted patiently, with an open, accommodating, and peaceful heart. As what I have experience from my anger problem for years, I could feel anger boiling and I know it unreasonable to get me upset but still I could not control it. This kind of feeling make me scared because I used to threaten people, until I learned to control anger. If you do not know how to control anger, you must learn - both for your own sake and the sake of those around you.

Many different strategies and skills for anger management intervention have been tried and tested. Some of the most empirically supported interventions are cognitive-behavioral interventions including relaxation coping skills, cognitive interventions, behavioral coping and social skills training, and problem-solving skills training. The goal of anger management is to reduce both your emotional feelings and the physiological arousal that anger causes. You can't get rid of, or avoid, the things or the people that enrage you, nor can you change them, but you can learn to control your reactions. And I found out that, as you can see it on the news regarding American drivers, named Adam Sandler and Jack Nicholson. Even persons have a controlling anger, granted that some are worse compared to others, but humans do harbor anger issues. Some of them keep on battle and negatively affect their health with anger on regular basis still it is essential to deal with them. Some ways you can do this are through meditation, therapy, physical activity and mental imagery. Obviously anger management therapy is a commonly known treatment for controlling anger.

Though, not everyone is open enough to obtain such aid, with proper meditation allow you to relax your mind and body, clear all the burdens and negativity. This is healthy and will reduce your feelings of anger. The idea of using hypnosis or meditation to control anger has grown in popularity recently. No one took the idea seriously at all. Everyone thought that you had to deal with anger intellectually. Anything that relaxes you emotionally, such as meditation, taking a long walk, taking a hot shower, or reading, can be a good method of controlling anger.

One thing here is physical venting this is one of my favorite in controlling anger. This involve through games such as basketball, rock climbing, swimming, martial arts, running or weight training. These great physical activities can vent feelings of anger at the end of your workout. The important thing is to find out what works for you and to do it!

Unfortunately, controlling anger is easier said and done. There are many methods out there nowadays, but none of them work for everyone. And there are several ways you can learn to control your anger. Relaxation is one of the best stress and anger management techniques. You can learn to relax through meditation, guided imagery, deep breathing, and hypnosis. When employing any of these techniques, you will be able to relax and calm down whenever you feel your temper getting the best of you. I found out that the best result from combining these two techniques which is anger management and anger therapy is we can learn tips and tricks to control our anger before it boils over and the have both good ways in controlling anger.

Another way of controlling anger here is once we fully

accept other people as they are without the slightest judgment or reservation - as all the enlightened beings accept us - then there is no basis for problems in our relations with others. Problems do not exist outside our mind, so when we stop seeing other people as problems they stop being problems. The person who is a problem to a non-accepting mind does not exist in the calm, clear space of patient acceptance.

Do you find yourself having to resort to shouting or anger to get your point across? Do you feel that others rub you up the wrong way and as a result you lose your temper and go 'out or control'? Do you feel that sometimes you can go just a little too far? If so then you need to consider getting some help... and fast! In this hectic age that we live in, more and more people are finding it increasingly more difficult to manage their anger. This is due to many reasons; however there are some things that are the same for everyone. Increasingly over the last few years, hypnosis has become a well-accepted way to get the help that you need for anger

Anger is an emotion that each one of us has experienced at some pint of our lives. Anger can be caused from worry, stress, fear, fatigue or bad thoughts. There are five dimensions of anger that are cognition, emotion, affect, communication and behavior. These five dimensions of anger can seem uncontrollable for many people. When someone is out of control their anger can actually become unstoppable.

Uncontrollable anger is extremely dangerous. Some people lose their temper and experienced such high levels of anger that they harm another individual. Anger can not only hurt someone else but can cause the person who experienced the flash of anger to get into trouble with the law. Anger is an emotion that is controllable. A person that experiences outbursts or rages of anger should consider anger management.

Hypnosis is an effective tool for anger management. Hypnosis is a type of soothing therapy that is safe, gentle and positive. That's the way hypnosis works in on a subconscious level.

Someone who is undergoing hypnosis will be put into a state of deep relaxation. It is during this state of deep relaxation that the subconscious mind is the most open to new ideas and perspectives. As the state of relaxation continues the individual, undergoing hypnosis, will receive positive suggestions. These positive suggestions include motivational encouragement, confidence-building statements and a set plan to control anger. Hypnosis will help to alleviate the stress and anxiety one feels while increasing self-esteem and confidence, thus aiding anger management.

One who has undergone hypnosis will experience a new thinking and behavior patterns. These new patterns are what allow a person to finally control their anger and to reach a healthy level of anger management.

Anger a valid emotion. You have a right to feel anger. The problem is not the emotion of anger but the effect of it on you and those around you. When you think about your anger, what is its function in your life? Does it keep people at arm's length and has a protective role or is it more sinister, is it a reflection of how you feel about yourself - low self-worth, low self-esteem and when you feel anger you are really angry with yourself? If frustration is part of your anger, the frustration is a signal to yourself that you can be better and yet you just keep the status quo.

How does your anger manifest itself? Do you lash out at others, verbally and/or physically? Do you enjoy the power from people being afraid of you? If you are reading this, you know that deep down this is not the way you want to be. You know you are capable of being a different better person without fear of showing all your emotions. I wonder how many times you have tried to change but you know others don't believe change is possible and when you don't receive benefits for changing, you just fall back into old ways.

What are the beliefs you hold about yourself? Do you feel that the world expects you to be an angry man/woman?

When anger is repressed, it is accompanied by self-destructive thoughts and a feeling of dissatisfaction. The loss of self-esteem is of central importance to those suffering from depression (repressed anger can lead to depression). Boys are taught to release their anger and girls are taught it is the social norm to contain their anger. Both sexes may repress their anger to such an extent that becomes people pleasers or "smiles" - without any outward sign of what they truly feel. With hypnosis, in a relaxed state, the client learns three things necessary for those with repressed anger issues: how to relieve the anger, change their trigger thoughts and be assertive. A feeling of inadequacy related to low self-esteem can add to the anger. It is a never ending cycle of negative thoughts, feelings of hostility inside with the stress of a happy facade which can eat the sufferer up inside.

If you deny your anger what physical manifestations does it produce? Headaches, pains and aches, irritable bowel syndrome can be caused as a result of repressed anger and stress. How was angered demonstrated in your home. Sometimes we can either mirror our parents or do the opposite. Your anger can be more a reflection on how you feel about yourself - feelings of inferiority, not being quite good enough but with gentle reprogramming you can improve your self-esteem. When you are really angry at someone, are you truly angry at them or do they remind you of someone from your past that made your angry or are you projecting your anger at yourself onto someone else. If your anger has ever caused you to lash out physically at someone or an animal, then you need to address why inflicting fear or physical pain on someone gives you a release.

While it would be lovely for this inner anger to be magically swept away, it is not possible to remove this repressed anger until we know what function it has. All habits, emotions have a role to play and if we leave a gap without knowing what caused the emotion in the first place, then something worse could take its place. Once we identify the function of the repressed anger, we can discover better, more positive ways of behaving. The life you want for yourself where you can feel truly happy and content, with a new assertiveness has to be more exciting to you than the live you are living now - at all emotional and physical levels. We need to understand the neurology of the mind. You know that repressing anger is just as bad as lashing out physically - someone is getting hurt either emotionally or physically. With hypnosis you can learn how to break the unwanted habit of not standing up for oneself while feeling the full force of the anger inside and develop a new connection of self-assertion without holding on to anger, without anger even developing. What different would this make to your life, what difference would it make to those around you, family and friends. Before making the change, you must take a detailed look at your life, what is the cost of staying the same and what will you gain by making the change - get ready to improve your life with hypnosis?

YOUR THOUGHTS AND THEIR POWER

Is there a little voice in your head that's holding you back? What if the words you heard can give you a boost instead of it weighing you down?

We all have the tendency to hold on to negative self-judgments no matter what status we hold in our society. Whether we are a high-ranking corporate executive who's at the helm of his career, or a successful entrepreneur reaping the rewards of his hard work, negative thoughts hold on to us. Along with, the constant stress, worry, and anxiety that we experience in our daily lives, nobody is spared from the plethora of distractions around us. Even when steeped in just reading a book, our mind wanders about 20% of the time. We have a difficult time being right here at the present moment.

Having negative thoughts are normal. Staying there is what causes most of the damage. Excessive mind wandering and self-criticizing can cause pain, anger, frustration, and fear that often leads to depression. It promotes the release of cortisol, a chemical substance that suppresses the immune system, and if ignored can result in ill health and even sickness. These will prevent you from enjoying life as you should.

In switching to a more positive thought pattern, you create space to invite anything you want into our life, like love, gratitude, excitement, and positivity. Acceptance allows you to be at peace and live your life to the fullest.

Thoughts are things, and your body is in fact a very powerful electromagnetic transmitter and receiver of energy of all kinds. Every single thought that befaces you will have a powerful impact on all the cells in your body. Positive or high vibrational thoughts can rid your body of disease and negative or low vibrational thoughts can give your body disease.

Stress, which can be defined as negative thoughts, cause the body to become acidic, an environment which enables and "feeds" all types of illnesses. These thoughts can be conscious or unconscious in nature and many of these negative thoughts are "trapped" in stressful or traumatic incidences that we experienced in our past. It has been documented that doctors have found the vast majority of people with cancer have had an incident in their past that caused tremendous grief, as individuals who have experienced heart attacks have been found to have suppressed anger. There is definite correlation between certain emotions and certain diseases.

The stress of living in today's world is higher than any other time in history. Driving a car today raises stress levels in the body to 1,000 times normal levels and add to it the use of a cell phone while driving a car today and the stress levels raise to 5,000 times normal levels. You become what you think about ...positive thoughts and low amounts of stress create an alkaline pH in the body which means you virtually cannot get sick and negative thoughts and emotions and high levels of stress cause the body to become acidic, leading to illness and disease.

Can you get rid of negative thoughts? We all have negative thoughts. In fact, we think of them more often than we should. When we are facing difficult situation, all we could think about are the negative outcomes. Our mind is flooded with doubts, worry, fear, guilt, and anger which not only cause us stress, but also affects our emotions and how we deal with others. And if we dwell on our negative thoughts and emotions, we attract the abundance of them which only worsen our situation. Our thoughts are so powerful, it can change the way we see ourselves and our perspective of life.

By just stopping yourself from thinking negative thoughts, you are merely suppressing them and it will come into a head when the same situation occurs. Negative thoughts are self-defeating and it is not enough to just ignore it because it won't change the fact that you are still harboring them. What you need is to replace them with positive ones. Here are some of the ways you can try to take control of your thoughts:

Be aware of your thoughts. If you find yourself thinking negatively, don't entertain it because it causes physical and mental stress. Sure, you are in times of distress so you can't help but think negatively about things but participating in them will not change anything but will only delay success and it will shorten your life because it will damage your immune system. Remember, you attract the things you are constantly thinking about. So once you start having negative thoughts, try to change the image in your mind and change it into something calming, and uplifting. Negative thoughts and self-talk is like some kind of self-hypnosis programming you for failure. Make it habit to think, "I can" instead of "I can't" or "It will," instead of "it won't". Whatever your thoughts are, just be sure to turn it into positive.

Change your focus - It's inevitable to have negative thoughts but the moment you dwell on them, you will only make matters worst than they already are. Channel your energy into positive and relax perspective so that you will be more receptive to see more opportunities. Surround yourself with circumstance and people who have positive orientation. Meditate or exercise because this will not only change your focus, this will also give you good health. You don't have to change your personality, just remember that nobody wants to be with someone who is grumpy and negative.

Getting rid of your negative thoughts is not easy so take it one step at a time. Once you have made a habit of it, your life will turn the way you wanted it to be. Positive thoughts create positive emotions and you will attract the abundance of positive experience.

Self hypnosis works by using two basic techniques: visualisation and hypnotic language. The former is a means of you expressing your desire to get rid of the negative thoughts preventing you from reaching your goal. The latter tool helps create the images and more through utilizing words and phrases in patterns to create images and to reinforce your goals. It is essential the two work together. If they do not, your goal will fall short.

Visualisation and hypnotic language have a single

goal. They are to guide you through the process of self hypnosis. In doing so, they lead you deep down into the level of your subconscious. This permits you to get to the heart of the problem. Your subconscious is behind your inability to reach your goal. It interferes with negative suggestions, cravings or derisive thoughts. Your subconscious does not permit you to believe you are what you want to become. Using hypnosis, you retrain your subconscious to accept and eventually embrace your vision of the new you.

The language is pre-recorded. While books do help you understand and may prove helpful in creating scripts for the pre-recorded material, the basis for your sessions are pre-recorded material. Whether you download these from your computer, buy some on line or in a retail specialty store or even prepare them yourself, this is an essential tool. You need them to guide you through and reinforce the process.

The pre-recorded material must consist of more than one option. While you need to select according to your goal e.g. non-smoker, you also need to have more than one appropriate recording. This provides variety from constant over repetition. It also allows you to build up towards your final goal. The material must always be positive in support of your goals. They need to be constantly reinforcing your decision and employ active and present verbs, words and phrases such as I am, I will and Now.

CHAPTER 13

HOW TO DEAL WITH GRIEF - 4 PROVEN STRATEGIES

So you have experienced the tragic loss of a loved one! May I extend my deepest sympathies to you in your time of sorrow. I offer below some effective techniques for How To Deal With Grief.

First, though, it is most important that you understand that you cannot "handle" or "manage" grief. It is not healthy or effective to try to manipulate grief or find a shortcut through it. There are, however, more comfortable ways to help you endure as the grief process unfolds.

1. Go With The Flow- In the early stages of your bereavement, do not try to hide it, suppress it or deny it. The best thing you can do is to let it in... let the grief wash over you at will and carry you along for now. Surrender to the grief to find your way through it. It is only later that you will find ways to put your grief aside in order to deal with the business of living... your job... your social life... your financial and legal affairs.

2. Postpone Decisions- Most mental health

professionals agree that you should try to put off major decisions for one year following a grievous loss. In other words, do not move, sell or buy real estate, marry or divorce, adopt or get pregnant if you can possibly avoid it... for one full year. Why? You just aren't in your right mind early in grief, and may make bad decisions you will sorely regret later. And about moving... don't... as one widow in a support group said... "It's best to grieve where things are familiar".

How to deal with grief...

3. Don't Grieve Alone- The funeral is over, out-of-town guests have gone home, and your friends seem to be getting back to their lives. You may be dismayed at this time to discover that you have been left alone to deal with your grief! Why does this happen? Where is everybody when you need them most? The truth is that most people, even friends and family, are not comfortable with grief. They don't know what to say or how to help... so they just stay away.

It is not healthy to grieve alone. So make the effort to find at least one friend or professional who does "get it". You need a supportive "ear" who will stand by you and let you express your grief without telling you it's "time to move on". You may even find it helpful at this point in your grief to join a grief support group in your area. This is a special kind of therapy that many have reported to be very helpful.

4. Be Gentle With Yourself- The best advice we can give you on how to deal with grief is this: be kind and gentle with yourself! Grief takes time and lots of hard work. Sadly, the only way through grief is directly. There are no shortcuts or easy ways to "handle" a healthy bereavement. So you must be patient and forgiving... of yourself.

This chapter has given you a few griefwork tips here, but there are many other proven methods for making grief more bearable and comfortable. Access more of these grief coping strategies from the resource box below.

CHAPTER 14
HOW TO DEAL WITH GRIEF HOLISTICALLY

By learning how to deal with grief, you are more than half way to resolving it. Why? Because the alternative is to swallow it, bury it deep, deny it. But you can't do that for long. You can't get away with denial. Sooner or later, it will resurface, only now as depression. In one way, that's really all you have to do, because the rest is likely to follow according to natural laws. Just by allowing is enough. Allow the tears. Allow the heart break. Allow the grief. By allowing, you are letting go.

If you don't have a past history of unresolved grief, this process is probably going to be quite quick. But the more you have stacked up, the more has to be released. And, as you are now allowing it to come out, it may all come tumbling out.

Which can be a bit overwhelming. But, as long as you know why it's happening, and continue to allow it, it will run it's course and go. Then you'll feel so much lighter. And you'll be so much healthier.

Without allowing this natural order of events, you can easily become stuck. And that's when you need help.

In my opinion, there is no better help for any problem than with homeopathy. Homeopathy works by clearing your blocks, by boosting your immune system. All done by supporting your body in what it is trying to achieve.

Suppression is a dirty word to homeopaths. Because you can't get away with suppression. One day it will come back. And in a different, but much worse form.

One of the most common homeopathic medicines for grief is Ignatia. This will work by defusing your grief and allowing that to dissipate. Without any effort on your part.

By learning how to deal with grief, you're going a long way to regain control of your health and so your life. The rest of the journey can only get better.

CHAPTER 15

HOW TO DEAL WITH GRIEF AND THE GRIEVING PROCESS

Grief isn't something that anyone wants to think about but it is a part of life that we all must face from time to time.

It is painful but it does have a purpose in our lives and can actually benefit us in many ways. Similarly to the way that the darkness of the night makes the brilliance of the morning light and sunrise so much more wonderful and amazing.

Grief works the same way in our lives, the dark and painful times can really help teach us to appreciate the beauty in the other times of life. Even in the midst our grief we can find so much more appreciation in the little things in life to be grateful for if will just look for it.

There are many different things in which we grieve over. Oftentimes the immediate thought of grief is the loss of a loved one and that is definitely a major source of grief.

Grief can come in many other forms: the loss of a

friendship, a friend moving away, a job loss, the loss of a dream, illness, moving to a new city, divorce, break up of a romantic relationship, loss of a pet, a life threatening situation, a natural disaster, and much more.

There are different ways in which we experience grief, there are even typical stages of grief. I have a BA degree in Psychology so I spent time studying the stages.

The interesting thing about grief and the stages is there is no correct way to go through the stages. Everyone experience the stages differently - and that is perfectly normal and okay.

One person may start with Anger while another person may find anger is the last stage they go through before Acceptance. Denial or Bargaining may be the first stage that they go through instead.

How freeing it is to realize that there is no wrong way to grieve! You don't have to feel bad about going through the process in an entirely different way than someone else who is grieving the same loss.

As humans it can be all too easy to look around at others going through the same experience and compare ourselves to them. It is natural to find yourself asking the following questions (and more!)...

* Am I sad enough?

* Am I too sad?

* Why am I this angry?

* Why am I not angry?

* Why am I hiding in work/hobbies/etc.?

* Why am I not responding the same way Bob is?

* I something wrong with me?

* What does everyone else think of how I'm grieving?

Regardless of how we deal with grief at least we can relax knowing that it's normal. (Assuming of course that we are not engaging in destructive behaviors such as abusing of alcohol, lashing out at loved ones, completely ignoring responsibilities, turning to drugs, harming yourself, etc. If that is the case then reaching out to someone is vital, whether it be a trusted friend or a professional.)

Grieving can be a very personal experience because it's something that we need to do in order to move past the loss and we can't experience in the same way that those near us who are grieving will experience it. But very often grieving follows similar patterns within the same person across different types of grief.

CHAPTER 16

HOW TO DEAL WITH GRIEF: ADJUSTING TO DEVASTATING LOSS

So many people underestimate the impact that grief has on their lives; they are flung into this nightmare and have no idea what to do or what is normal. They feel totally alien to themselves and can be completely overwhelmed by the intensity of their emotions and the impact which the loss has on their whole body, it affects them on every level.

When we are in such devastating pain, all we want are things the way they were. We want our life as it once was and our loved ones back with us. The intensity of the emotional pain is crippling as we wake up each day without them. We wonder how we'll ever get through this and how we'll deal with this pain, day in, day out. We want to know what to do next, how to cope and what we can do to feel better, to stop hurting so much.

Here are 3 key steps you can take right now to begin the process of adjusting to loss

- Express and feel your emotions: As much as it hurts, suppressing how you feel is like putting a lid on a pressure cooker and turning off the steam valve, eventually it will blow. By expressing your emotions, you start the healing process. Sometimes the emotions can be overwhelming so we might have to stage their release. Starting the ritual of taking time for daily writing can be one way to do this.

- Get support: It is so important that when we are grieving we have support. Say 'Yes' when people reach out. Finding out how others have adapted to loss can be so helpful in knowing that you too will get through this. Joining a grief support group can also be of tremendous value, either online or in person. Someone who has been through what you have is more likely to understand in many ways that others cannot. Utilise available resources, programmes and services to support you in your healing journey.

- Do what feels right for you: The experience of grief and loss is extremely personal and different for everyone. It can be totally all-consuming and pervade every part of your being to the exclusion of everything else. Other people may have no idea of the inner turmoil you are experiencing, or they are very well aware and meaning well, encourage you to do this or do that. It becomes critical that you consider yourself at this time. Listen to your heart, and do what feels right for you, even if it goes against family wishes or convention. Look after you.

CHAPTER 17
HOW TO DEAL WITH GRIEF IN A HEALTHY WAY

Everyone in their life at some point or another experiences grief. It could come through death for a loved one, finance tribles or possibly a relationship. Everyone on this planet experiences grief many times over.

What we must understand is that grief is a normal part of life, and is something that you cannot avoid. It's normal for us to try and avoid the feelings of grief as we usually don't know how to cope. The truth of the matter is, it never gets easier no matter how much grief you have experienced in your life.

Their are a few points that we should take into consideration when faced with any form of grief. Below I have listed these points for you to consider on how to cope with grief. This is a short 3 step process for anyone to follow:

1) First we must accept what causes us the personal grief we are going through. Self admittance that we are

experiencing grief rather than denial brings us closer to coping with grief.

2) We must analyze our actions and thoughts and come to a final conclusion to whether we contributed to the grieving in one form or another.

3) Lastly, once we have analyzed all other key points we then must start the process of overcoming our grief, their isn't a magical formula to cure grief instantly. Like anything in life, things need time.

With grief comes sadness, sadness leads to pain mentally and physically, depression and regret as well as suicide in rare cases. These are some of the things that accompany grief which sadly can't be avoided for some, the best we can do is find a way to soothe the process and move on with our lives. Always remember you are not alone, and whether you believe it or not time is the best healing that you could afford yourself. Start with the 3 key process and write down points on a daily basis that lead you to the feeling of grief, sadness, regret etc, then work on making small changes to reverse these feelings one step at a time.

If this seems too difficult for you don't fret, I advice consulting your local doctor and he/she will forward you to some sort of counseling as well as offer the support you may need in times of grief.

Always take action, don't let negative feeling take control of your life, you are the master and creator of all things on this planet. With time and action you will find that you can overcome anything, and each and passing day will make you stronger in the long run.

CHAPTER 18
HOW TO DEAL WITH STRESS AND DEPRESSION

When it comes to stress in our life, it is important to be able to accurately understand our stress levels, understand how we respond to stress, and develop effective ways to respond when stress levels get too high. Some stress is a good thing, keeping us alert and motivated. By triggering a burst of energy, stress can stimulate memory, help us to accomplish a task, or meet a challenge. Stress hormones increase with light exercise, or when we face the challenge of a test or deadline. Individuals vary in what they find beneficial or productive.

For some, meeting a challenge such as a ski run or performing before an audience is enjoyable; a different person may have an entirely different response. When we feel in control of a situation and gain a sense of accomplishment, we experience stress in a beneficial way. Stress is also a normal response when facing a critical situation. Normally, once the cause of stress is gone, the body's metabolism returns to normal.

However, chronic high levels of stress can result in continued elevated levels of stress hormones, where the body does not return to a normal relaxed state. It is this state of continued high level of stress, never really returning to normal, which will lead to physical and psychological problems that threaten our health and well-being.

According to the University of Maryland Medical Center, medical studies have shown that continued elevated levels of stress hormones may lead to anxiety or depression. When we feel overwhelmed by circumstances, we begin to experience a perpetual stress response.

This is especially true when circumstances are not in our control, or when a stressful situation is ongoing, such as a death in the family, accident or illness of a loved one, as a caregiver for someone with a conditions such as Alzheimer's, a job loss, financial difficulties - especially when compounded by lack of health insurance, domestic violence, or substance abuse by a family member.

Here are some tools you can use if you are wondering how to deal with stress and depression:

Food

A healthy diet is a powerful tool for health. But just what is a healthy diet? Which, among the barrage of diet recommendations, will help with stress and depression? Much of what is quick and easy to grab to eat when we are overtaxed and stressed is highly counterproductive. Some foods will boost serotonin, and are "comfort foods". Other foods cut the cortisol and adrenaline levels, reducing those stress hormones that trigger stress.

Carbohydrates are comfort foods, but need to be complex carbohydrates such as oatmeal, whole grain bread, pasta and cereal. Simple carbohydrates such as sugar and foods sweetened with fructose and corn syrup will destabilize the blood sugar and aggravate the effects of stress.

Magnesium is an important electrolyte that is essential to good muscle tone. A lack of magnesium will lead to muscle tension, resulting in the intensification of the stress response. Nuts and beans, whole grains, green leafy vegetables and seafood such as halibut and salmon are rich in magnesium. Epsom salt is magnesium sulfate, and a soak in a hot bath with two cups of Epsom salts is also a good way to relax the muscles and absorb magnesium.

A modern diet tends to be deficient in omega-3 fatty acids, which are essential fatty acids that are critical for a number of metabolic processes. Fatty fish, (not farm-raised; because of the low-omega-3 feed, farm-raised fish do not supply omega-3 fatty acids), flax seed oil, or supplement with fish oil or a combination fish and flax seed oils.

Herbal Supplements

Although more research is needed to verify effectiveness, two herbs show promise for their calming effect. The most researched is St. John's Wort; studies have shown this herb may relieve mild to moderate levels of depression. Valerian root has not been as well researched to date, but has a long history of use for its ability to reduce stress and tension.

Many holistic clinics recommend Valerian for the relief of muscle tension, which is a common condition with those under stress. As with any supplement, it is very important to always discuss the wisdom of using any herbal remedy with your health provider before using it, in order to understand any possible side effects and make sure there are no contraindications or interference with any medications you may be taking.

Mind and Body

While it may be difficult to summon the motivation to exercise and engage in mindfulness-based stress reduction practices, research has shown that these are very helpful in reducing stress and depression. Whether it is a workout at a gym or at home, a walk in nature, yoga, and tai chi are all effective by helping to support the health of mind and body. Spiritual practices such as meditation and prayer have also been proven to help cope with stress and depression.

Cognitive Behavioral Therapy

Because stress and depression are so debilitating, and often triggered by events outside of our control, getting the kind of help that will effectively address the issues is very important. Research is showing that cognitive behavioral therapy is one of the most effective strategies for dealing with stress and depression. Dr. Esther Sternberg, M.D., chief of neuroendocrine immunology ad behavior at the National Institute of Mental Health is a top stress researcher. In an article by Karen Bruno, reviewed by Lauren J. Martin, M.D., on WebMD, she states: "It is important that people suffering from depression not blame themselves - it's partly your genetic makeup, partly your current environment, and partly your early environment that led to the depression. If you're depressed, seek help. You can't beat it on your own."

CHAPTER 19

HOW TO DEAL WITH PANIC ATTACKS WITH ONE SIMPLE IDEA

Panic attack sufferers know far too well just how horrible the experience can be. For those of us with this disorder, learning how to deal with panic attacks can be difficult since there's so much information on the subject. Recently I've come across a unique perspective on why people get these attacks, and how you can use this information to overcome them.

Perhaps the most common treatment for panic attacks is prescribed medication. These come in a variety of types, SSRI's, beta blockers, tricyclic antidepressants, just to name a few. Although these have all shown an effectiveness in treating panic, what they all have in common is a rather long list of side-effects. As well, most coping techniques were designed in the late 70's, and are incredibly out of date. You should also take into account that these forms of treatment really only mask the problem, without ever actually solving them.

So, figuring out how to deal with panic attacks can be a challenge, especially since every popular method seems to not necessarily work for all people.

The one simple idea I mention in the topic is something that I discovered recently that's very unique to the way most methods are used for treating panic attacks. You see, the very definition of panic disorder is the fear of having an attack. Because of this, we get locked in a loop of anxiety. The initial attack, fear of the next one, until we eventually have thc next one.

Panic feeds off of fear. It's the fuel that keeps it coming time and again. We must learn how to cut the fuel, the fear, in order to break free of the cycle.

Learning how to deal with panic attacks doesn't need to be as difficult as it's made out to be. You can overcome them by using this concept. Learn why you fear them, overcome the fear, and live a panic free life.

CHAPTER 20

FAITH AT WORK - HOW TO DEAL WITH JOB LOSS IN A FAITH-CENTERED WAY

Millions of people have lost their jobs as a result of this recession. You may be one of them. While the stock market has shown some positive movement, it's unclear whether things will genuinely improve soon or if the rally we've seen is a false one.

So how does a person of faith deal with the loss of their job and not lose their faith?

Each of us truly does grieve differently because we move through the stages differently and that movement may not be in a straight line. We may bounce around a bit between some of the stages and we may zip through one or two of them. The objective is to deal effectively with each stage and to work through them so we don't get stuck in any one of them.

Shock. "What?" No matter how aware we've tried to be about our company's financial health and our own job security hearing the words "...and we're going to have to let you go..." still comes as a shock to some degree. We may be listening to what's being said but it may be difficult for our brain and our ears to work together. After the meeting is over you may realize later you didn't ask any of the dozens of questions you have. You may not even remember what exactly was said to you. It's OK to go back and ask for clarification later.

Denial. "This can't be happening to me," is a common reaction and it often goes through your mind while listening to your supervisor explain the separation process. Ask for all the information about your separation in writing. Your company should have these documents prepared ahead of time. Make sure you get them so you're able to review them later as your ability to focus improves.

Anger. "After all I've done for this place?!" It can be difficult to believe that after the tough projects success-fully completed, the deadlines met, and other accomplishments, you suddenly find out your expenda-ble. It hurts. It's not fair. And we react with anger as we try to make sense of it and protect our battered ego. While your feelings are justified (and we can always find a reason to justify our feelings, can't we?) anger is a dangerous emotion. As it wells up and spills over it can be easy for us to then lose control of our words and actions. Be very careful at this time. Even if you weren't happy at your job you'll want to obtain a good reference and be among those who are called back if the situation changes. People won't remember that your anger was justified; they'll just remember how angry you got. As a former recruiter I can tell you your anger can come out in a job interview and it doesn't help you sell yourself to a future employer.

It's also easy for us to be angry with God. You're a nice person...a person of faith. How can He let this happen to you? Unfortunately we use earthly things to measure God's love for us. He doesn't.

Bargaining. "I'll be a better person if you let me find a job, God." As the search for a job begins and in some cases drags on you may find yourself trying to negotiate with the Lord in an attempt to get what you want. We've all done this at various times in our lives. Instead of promising to do something if God gives you what you want, try just doing what you promise. If it's that you'll go to church more often if He gives you a job how about just going to church more often no matter what?

Sometimes making an alternate offer to our employer may actually be a good idea. Offering to work a reduced schedule or even be available for projects or part time work can provide you with some additional income while you look for a new position. It can also demonstrate incredible flexibility and the kind of positive outlook that's valued even if it isn't accepted.

Depression. "Why have you forsaken me?" With newspapers full of stories about business closings, executive excess, and more job losses it's easy to become emotionally overwhelmed by this economic crisis. Add to that stress of going on interviews and not being selected and it's easy to hear the voice of negativity convincing you that you're worthless and will never find a job. This is the most dangerous point of all and it can be easy to fall deeper and deeper into this black hole where we become paralyzed by our feelings of sadness.

God hasn't forsaken you. Business and personal coach Duke Clarke points out that our definition of "prosper" and God's are two different definitions. Duke says, "The biblical definition for "prosper" is to achieve what you set out to do as explained in Genesis when Abraham sent his servant to find a wife for his son. So be sure to define your prosperous living in light of the richness of your whole life and not just based on income." God loves you no matter what. Focus on and celebrate the simple, joyful pleasures we have every day.

Testing. "Please God let this work." Perhaps it's a retraining program you've qualified for, a temporary job you've gotten, or a consulting project you've been awarded. At some point you may dip your toe in a new pool of experiences, testing the waters of a new venture and a new way of working. It's easy to be fearful at this point. As adults we're quick to label less than perfect results as "failures" or "mistakes" when in fact it's simply part of moving forward and learning something new. Sometimes we can get a bit frenetic in our testing, constantly trying something new without giving any one activity a chance to build up steam.

Acceptance. "I think this is going to work out." Suddenly it begins to dawn on you that your new circumstances are full of benefits. Whether it's having fun making meals together to save money, or growing closer by really discussing how to deal with the financial challenges, or discovering you really can teach an old dog new tricks, when you reach a point of accepting the new direction your life is moving things become easier as you swim with the tide rather than against it.

It's easy to get caught up in any one of the stages before you arrive at acceptance. Worry can easily consume us. Being a person of faith doesn't mean we won't go through challenging and sad times. It means understanding that God is with us to guide and strengthen us as we maneuver around these obstacles. Just as a gem starts as a rock and must be tossed and tumbled to come out brilliant and beautiful in the end, our struggles do the same for us when faith and prayer become a part of our rejuvenation process.

Here are 5 practical things to do to help not to loose faith or heart in this time:

Take time. Give yourself time to feel the pain and sadness of what you're experiencing. Review the separation details your company provides and investigate all of the company, state, and federal benefits due you. Many people discover this is really a gift in disguise. Think about what you didn't like about your job and reflect on what you'd most enjoy doing now. How can you make that happen?

Take care. Whether you want to admit it or not you're in a fragile state. Eat healthfully. Get exercise. Pray often. Limit your exposure to bad news and to those of your friends and family who tend to focus on the negative. While sympathy is appreciated, constantly listening to variations of "ain't it awful" will only reinforce negativity in your mind and heart.

Take action. Movement is rejuvenating and empowering. Develop a schedule and stick to it. Set a timer and focus chunks of time on your job search. Take a 15 minute break to do some simple task like laundry, then set the timer again and do more job search work. Research companies, find training programs, write cover letters.

Give to others. You'll soon have learned quite a bit as you navigate the forest of the job search process in your area. You can give helpful advice to others in your church who are newly unemployed. Speak to your pastor about creating a support group. Find a charity you believe in and volunteer. Help at the local animal shelter where caring for God's helpless creatures will be much appreciated. Studies have shown animals have a soothing effect on people. It's free stress therapy. Volunteering is a great way to meet others who could possibly help you find a new job. It's also a wonderful way to take your mind off of yourself as you help others overcome their challenges.

Talk to those who can help. God made us as social animals. Most of us need other people and talking through our problems helps us tremendously. Find those willing to listen who don't just provide a sympathetic ear but who are able to give useful advice, direct you to resources, and help you smile.

CHAPTER 21

HOW TO RECOVER FROM FAILURE - HOW TO DEAL WITH YOUR FAILURE MORE PRODUCTIVELY

In the modern society we're living in today, many of us treat failure as an embarrassment. This notion has been wedged in our minds since childhood. We have never been taught how to deal with failure objectively and productively, neither from our parents or teachers in school.

For example, you have just received an email from a company you had a job interview with last week. The email informs that you've not been selected for the job. Now, most people will view this as total failure on their part. But, do you really fail? Is it fair to view such situation as a total failure?

I think not if you can try to look at the situation from a more positive angle. Ask yourself these questions... are you a total failure? Or is it just your performance/skills that make you fail? These questions allow you to view the issue in a better perspective. If it's my performance/skill that lets me down, how can I improve upon it?

See the difference? If you can calm yourself down and view your issue positively, you will be able to deal with it more objectively and productively. You will treat the failure as a learning opportunity to improve yourself.

NEVER EVER think that you fail as a person. This can plunge your self-esteem into the lowest level and make you feel very depressed. You will start to label yourself as a failure and generalize this to other situations.

You see, failure is not a permanent condition, it's merely a jugdement from a view or an event. Instead of labelling or blaming yourself as a total failure, look at the causes of the failure. Most common causes of failure can be eliminated.

For example, one of the most common causes of failure is poor social or interpersonal skills. And since these are "skills", they can be acquired and hence the causes can be eliminated. Some of the most important social skills are:

- being sensitive to other's feelings

- being empathetic and sympathetic

- being emotionally stable

- able to listen to others empathetically

- able to understand how people feel and how groups function

- able to give directions clearly and effectively

- able to give constructive criticism

- able to take criticism constructively

Note that all these are skills that can bc learned, practiced and improved.

Of course, there are many more causes of failure; which is beyond the scope of this article to discuss all. The main message I want you to learn from this chapter is to learn how to deal with failure more productively. Do not fear failure and do not label yourself as a failure.

All successful people are able to learn from their mistakes, give themselves an opportunity to survive the defeat and come out to be tougher and more resilient to face life challenges more effectively. As the saying goes... "Failure is the first step to success."

CHAPTER 22
HOW TO DEAL WITH DISAPPOINTMENT

Disappointment is a killing feeling we know too well. It is a feeling of sinking in the heart, body, mind and soul. You literally feel your energy level goes down gradually, until it almost touches your feet. It feels like sadness merged with bits of anger. It can be described as the antonym of anticipation, like anticipation gone bad.

Eliza Tabor once said: "Disappointment to a noble soul is what cold water is to burning metal; it strengthens, tempers, intensifies, but never destroys it." I like this quote because it gives us hope, that even though disappointment cools/ kills off our passion in one instant, the result it produces is to our benefit, more strength. It is such an unpleasant feeling yet it seems inevitable sometimes. Yet, who said it was a bad thing? It happens frequently and commonly, and almost no one is immune to it. However, the more we overcome disappointment, the more capable we are of dealing with it, and the more resourceful we become in seeking alternatives. So what causes disappointment to hit our brains and hearts, and robs us illusion and excitement? Most importantly, how can we avoid it from happening over and over again?

People are creatures of habit. They're creatures of hope and anticipation too, especially when it regards a personal matter that they really want to attain. Therefore, out of the eagerness to get to a certain goal, we start building hopes to get to them, and some of us - through imagination - may even start feeling they're there already, which is not a wrong thing to do per se. Yet, one cannot deny that dwelling in such mental and emotional state is a type of illusion. One creates an illusion and believes it. The defining line then between illusion and turning it into reality is whether or not one commits to a set of actions that lead them to achieving their illusion.

Most self-help books promote such practice, and even go on to describe it as the formula or "the Secret" for achieving our goals. Yet, how many of us would try what those books say and believe entitled already of the privileges sometimes even in the middle of the road to achieving their goals. When passion gets triggered in our hearts, our levels of excitement rise to unprecedented levels, and we feel we want to act upon this immense positive energy. Sure, optimism and positive thinking are key in stimulating the brain to try to generate a productive perspective on matters, and therefore, not surrender to failure or bitterness resulting from feeling disappointed upon experiencing a constant failure.

When imagination starts generating more passion, which - in turn- triggers intrinsic motivation in individuals, they charge people to reach their goals with maximum force and without a single moment of hesitation. That can be described as action-upon-passion. This can be visible in cases where one falls in love; he/ she is capable of going all lengths to get to what they want.

On the other hand, while there's nothing wrong with acting-upon-passion, but pausing to think every once in a while is a key element in the formula of success. The notion of going forward without a pause is commonly believed to be productive, especially if it was producing favorable results. On the other hand, going on without a stop is like asking a car to run non-stop without gas. Not stopping to assess the current situation is a mistake we often make, especially following a dense period of thinking or production.

The Need To Pause During Action

Circumstances change, new surprises emerge, and if we keep looking forward without moving our eyes around to have a complete perspective on our current surrounding, we may then become oblivious to any influences, factors or disturbances that may hinder us from achieving our goals. New learning is formed of the current obstacle, and a healthy brain starts generating other possible ways of going around that obstacle. However, this depends on whether one sees things from negative or a positive perspective, which also dictates their level of productivity as result. The more negative a person's thoughts are, the more prone to disappointment this person is. Certainly, disappointment is a very unproductive place to be per se, but the knowledge forming from it is what determines its usefulness.

For instance, a man sets out to arrive to work early, as this is important to his entire department, and helps him score high in his boss' eyes. While driving along, his car breaks down or has an accident. Clearly, there are several ways of looking at this hindrance; one of which is very common, i.e. one is unlucky.

One may say to oneself:

- I'm unlucky, and this is gonna be a very bad day for me from the looks of it. I wonder why I am not as lucky as others are!

- I'm hopeless. Although I have left particularly early this morning, I will still be late. If it's not my own delay, something else happens to make sure that I'm late. What are they going to say about me at work.

- Life is always against me. All people go to work every day, but life just chooses me out of everybody else to get an accident or have a blown tire!

- I must've been envied by others because I am such a high achiever at work. I must be careful of all those evil-eyes at work! Mark said I had a great car the other day! He must've envied me for having such a fast and reliable car that gets me to work every day on time.

This way of negative self-talk or 'self-suggestion' (as Napoleon Hill calls it in his book "Think & Grow Rich") creates disappointment along with a list of other negative feelings and thoughts. All previous monologues carry the potential of setting ourselves for disappointment, anger, fear, doubt, resentment, etc. They certainly are unproductive as they promote self-limitation, self-doubt, misery, feeling victimized, etc.

Other possible ways of looking at the same situation:

- It's OK. These things happen. I'm not the only person with a blown tire. Let me call Melissa to tell her I'm gonna be a bit late today.

- It was very important to me to arrive to work early today, but it's OK. Better arrive late but safe than fast but sorry.

- I have to keep making the effort to arrive early at work. It's important to me and to the people at work, especially my boss.

Self-suggestion is a crucial dynamism, by which we constantly construct our self-image in our minds. If it is influenced by negative thoughts, it may pollute our self-image with unproductive traits, which lead to disappointment eventually, which then feeds self-loathing into the vicious cycle.

If we see ourselves or others as a failure, we are bound to be disappointed by ourselves or others.

Hesitation and Delay

One may quickly judge hesitation and delay as disappointing acts. One may also think they are obstacles in the way of moving forward. As a matter of fact, when we find ourselves suddenly hesitating to make a certain action, of which we had been contemplating for a while, it may just be the most appropriate step for us to do. In addition, we may spare ourselves the disappointment of a possible failure resulting from committing that action, or from not stopping to think about it while acting upon it. Hesitation in this sense offers an opportunity for further assessment of the current situation, which may well save us from a possible disappointment, had we committed the action we had set to do.

How can delay be useful? I heard someone say yesterday that delay is a good thing too, because it allows one to re-evaluate one's expectations and take on things. It also reminds us why we went on to do a certain thing, or why we thought of someone in a particular way. The longer we heighten our awareness around the details of the current situation, the clearer our vision becomes. This way, even though delay may be a disappointing act by itself, it may still be to our benefit, as our re-assessment of the situation shall provide better clarity.

How To Deal With Disappointment:

Following are some tips that can help us deal with disappointment in a productive way, as opposed to the unproductive habits people usually fall for, like complaining, whining, silence, lack of action, etc.

- When you are in a situation and you feel disappointed of yourself or others, stop and take time to understand why you feel and think that way. Consider whether you -

in the first place - had formed realistic expectations around yourself or someone else. Consider why you had those expectations, what went wrong that led you to feel disappointed, and how can you better improve your expectations next time.

- If you plan on doing something or committing to a certain action, like dieting or studying, and then you got distracted or disconnected from doing that, do not surrender to the quick trap of blaming yourself and saying how disappointed you are of yourself. It doesn't lead you any where but to the place where you are. So in order to achieve your goals, you need to pause for a while, think, re-assess the whats, hows and whys and then commit to following your objectives with the new expectations in mind.

- If you set out to do something and your interrupted by a failure or an annoyance (something outside your control), don't succumb to thinking that it's destiny playing against you, and constantly sabotaging your progress. Don't blame anyone for surprises or new experiences. You simply didn't know what you learned later, so take it easy, deal with it and move on.

- Always check in with yourself, visualizing a table of three columns in your head, categorizing your Thoughts,

Actions, and Feelings separately from one another, to better be able to raise your awareness around what it is exactly that is making you feel disappointed, how it happened and why. Then, you can start thinking of better ways of handling the new situation.

- Follow your intuition, even if that meant your feeling disappointed in yourself or somebody being disappointed in you, because you hesitated or delayed saying or doing something. Your larger self is wiser than your existential self, so follow its lead.

- Always remember who you are at the end of the day, and what is your life purpose at the end of your life. Trust that and act upon this wisdom. It is who you are and why you do things the way you do. Also, it's a much more peaceful place than self-loathing.

Disappointment is a very unpleasant place to be, and if we settle with it, we are only blocking ourselves from more productive actions that can be learned from that disappointing situation. Therefore, raise your awareness around the details of it and set new action steps to handle it. No one is perfect, and certainly neither are you. So take it easy, embrace life with all its challenges, and surmount them with determination and faith that one way or another, you will eventually get what you want to achieve.

CONCLUSION

Getting stressed out and over worked are the main possibilities in our life. Both these possibilities could happen every single day. Access to information and people is very important, but this may sometimes make a person feel stressed out. To maintain a balanced level of the stress we take, we need to relax each day for an appropriate time period. This enhances the way your body, mind and spirit works.

As we need to maintain a balanced diet, we also need to maintain a balance between stress and relaxation. If a person takes stress and does not relax his body, then life would be adversely affected by it. Stress causes our heart rate to speed up, increase in heavy breathing and blood pressure. Stress causes heart diseases, chest pains, headaches, high blood pressure and can even affect our digestive system. Feeling overworked and tired is as unhealthy as obesity. If somebody figures out that he is being stressed out he should go use relaxation as a proper diet to maintain the level of stress.

Techniques:

Breathing is the most immediate technique of relaxation. When you feel stressed out, take deep breaths and lower your breathing to decrease high heart rate and decrease excessive blood pressure. Shut your eyes to eradicate visual stress and to increase the attention towards breathing. Use your imagination to travel to peaceful and quite places. If an individual wants to increase their meditation skills, one should try yoga and Tai Chi. These will increase awareness in our body.

Exercise can even get rid of stress. Exercise will release mind depression and keeps an individual smiling all the time. Massage is a great way to release stress. It will help your mind to remain calm. For those people who say the best medicine is laughter are hundred percent right. Laughing helps in deep breathing. This increases circulation to the body and lowers endorphins.

To maintain proper health, you need to relax for a quality period of time. Use a peaceful area in your home to relax, exercise and meditate. Listen to soothing music and ask your family members to give you a body massage. Use a hammock in your yard or garden to sway. This really relaxes the mind as when a person sways under natural air, he feels highly at ease. You can read a novel or listen to some music which will divert your mind from any thoughts that causes you to take tension and get stressed out. One of the main health problems that cause many major health issues is getting overworked. Relaxation will help you counter this major problem. Sleep at the appropriate time and then wake up at the right time. Maintain a good and healthy diet to keep your health under control.

Anger is an emotion which arises in response to any event which we may interpret as crossing our boundaries and attacking. We respond with anger when we feel that we need to defend ourselves physically, our family members or our country, our property, our values and even our entitlements. Anger is the response to attack when we can lose something, but also when we do not receive what we feel we deserve.

Anger is a prompt for attack as the best defense; the emotion is associated with biological changes in the body as the body prepares for combat, the stress enzymes are released, the blood pressure rises, the heart beats quicker, and we may feel hot and even start shaking. The biological changes can be very rapid when the strong anger arises, and it can quickly turn into a violent rage without much thinking. Sometimes the opposite happens, we mentally block the prolonged frustration and anger and the biological changes like high blood pressure and stress enzymes become permanent, leading to a serious health problems.

Anger is most often a secondary emotion, caused by fear, insecurity, low confidence, hurt and pain. When you are confident and secure, you do not need to respond with anger to critics or judgments. The words or actions of other people do not affect you when your self-esteem is strong, your feel your worth and you treat critics as getting a feedback and good tips to improve. Yes, when you are confident and open, you are grateful for critics, as it helps you to grow and learn.

Similarly, when we hold hurt and pain in our hearts, we are afraid of more hurt and pain, and we respond with anger when we feel that it may happen again. It is also easier to hold onto anger, because it makes us stronger to be angry than hurt and sad, and the old anger is revoked at any situation which reminds us of the old hurt. Those connections are on the subconscious level, very often not logical, difficult to trace.

We are also angry when we are denied the fulfillment of our desires. Some people are carrying anger and resentment from their younger years. Life is a challenge and has many needs. Baby cries with anger when it is hungry; little child will be angry when her sister has more attention from parents. Having more, accumulating goods, receiving awards etc makes us feel secure and important, and stronger. So again, the desires, the need to receive comes from basic insecurities and low confidence. The unreasonable anger when somebody receives more has also usually roots in the past. When we are free from this kind of desire, the need to grasp, the need to be special, the need to be better than others or have more, we are free not only from this sort of anger, we are free to use or potential to achieve more.

And there is also the primary anger, just a survival tool, which prompts us to action when we are in real danger, or there is a real danger to others, or our basic values are attacked. This kind of anger allows us to overcome the paralyzing fear so we can stand up for ourselves and defend our basic existence.

Anger management is about acknowledging and expressing your anger in an acceptable way. Uncontrolled anger creates problems, makes relationships difficult, can be damaging for us and for our surrounding, as it easily leads to abusive words or acts of violence, and even to the jail sentence. Denying the anger and suppressing it builds the pressure and leads to uncontrolled eruption when we cannot stand it anymore. It also affects health and brings other emotions, like guilt when we condemn ourselves for anger. It is better to express anger in a respectful way.

Anger management is also about understanding your anger and being able to prevent it in the first place by knowing the triggers and finding the ways to solve the situation before the anger arises. We can train ourselves to stay rational instead of letting the anger blind us out, so we can assess the situation and realize that we overact, that the threat is not real. We can learn relaxation techniques, as it is rather difficult to become angry when you are totally relaxed. We can learn many other ways to deal with strong emotions.

Hypnotherapy is the best tool for anger management, because it allows you to access your internal resources to find the best solutions to manage your anger. You can also implement your solutions in hypnosis and rehearse the challenging situations, still in hypnosis. This way the solutions are working on both conscious and subconscious levels, so it is like the automatic habit change. With hypnotherapy and some NLP techniques performed in hypnosis, we can also neutralize the triggers, so you will be much calmer in the situations which would normally bring anger.

Hypnotherapy also allows you to understand you anger better, by going not only to the current situations which bring anger, but also to the original events which are the reasons for the triggers. These events are usually forgotten, buried deep in subconscious mind. We can access them while in deep hypnosis and we can change the beliefs and perceptions of the past, because we can see it now with reason, through the adult eyes, not through the eyes of a frightened child. Once this is done, the anger dissolves, as the old triggers become neutral.

And we can do even more, much more than just managing the anger, we can create the real miracles in hypnosis. Hypnotherapy will help you to resolve the real reasons for anger, depression, anxiety and fear, insecurity, low confidence, hurt and pain or deep sadness. All those underlying emotions are often hidden deep in the subconscious mind and are difficult to trace. With hypnotherapy, we can access the subconscious mind and solve the anger by dealing with and letting go the causes of underlying emotions. As a result, we are more confident, relaxed, stronger and happier, so we do not need to be angry anymore.

REFERENCES

The emotional syndrome 1997 Odufuwa Seyi

https://www.nhs.uk/conditions/cognitive-behavioural-therapy-cbt/

Kingdon, David; Price, Jessica (April 17, 2009). "Cognitive-behavioral Therapy in Severe Mental Illness." Psychiatric Times. 26 (5).

https://www.psychologytoday.com/intl/basics/cognitive-behavioral-therapy

https://www.mayoclinic.org/tests-procedures/cognitive-behavioral-therapy/about/PAC-20384610'https://www.mayoclinic.org/tests-procedures/cognitive-behavioral-therapy/about/pac-20384610

https://www.verywellmind.com/what-is-cognitive-behavior-therapy-2795747

Kingdon, David; Price, Jessica (April 17, 2009). "Cognitive-behavioral Therapy in Severe Mental Illness". Psychiatric Times. 26 (5).

https://www.medicalnewstoday.com/articles/296579.php

Do not go yet; One last thing to do

If you enjoyed this book or found it useful I'd be very grateful if you'd post a short review on it. Your support really does make a difference and I read all the reviews personally so I can get your feedback and make this book even better.

Thanks again for your support!

www.ingramcontent.com/pod-product-compliance
Lightning Source LLC
Chambersburg PA
CBHW061755250726
48657CB00001B/135